IT'S ALL GOOD

The Road to Living Peacefully

Spiritual Vision

Dan Costello

IT'S ALL GOOD
THE ROAD TO LIVING PEACEFULLY

Copyright © 2021 Dan Costello.

All rights reserved. No part of this book may be used or reproduced by any means, graphic, electronic, or mechanical, including photocopying, recording, taping or by any information storage retrieval system without the written permission of the author except in the case of brief quotations embodied in critical articles and reviews.

iUniverse books may be ordered through booksellers or by contacting:

iUniverse
1663 Liberty Drive
Bloomington, IN 47403
www.iuniverse.com
844-349-9409

Because of the dynamic nature of the internet, any web addresses or links contained in this book may have changed since publication and may no longer be valid. The views expressed in this work are solely those of the author and do not necessarily reflect the views of the publisher, and the publisher hereby disclaims any responsibility for them.

Any people depicted in stock imagery provided by Getty Images are models, and such images are being used for illustrative purposes only.
Certain stock imagery © Getty Images.

ISBN: 978-1-6632-0928-3 (sc)
ISBN: 978-1-6632-0927-6 (e)

Library of Congress Control Number: 2021919910

Print information available on the last page.

iUniverse rev. date: 12/27/2021

"It is true that sometimes all is not well, but what remains is "always Good."

Once I chose a spiritual path, I began to see a world in which all was created equal, and events, people, and things were opportunities to experience love and render blessings. It was the same world but now seen through new eyes.

CONTENTS

A Message from Three Angels ix
Preface xi
Introduction xv

Chapter 1   Listening to Life 1
Chapter 2   Neutral Witness 10
Chapter 3   Sacred Journey 18
Chapter 4   Duality 26
Chapter 5   Surrender 32
Chapter 6   Hidden Teachings 44
Chapter 7   Unconditionality 53
Chapter 8   Handling Fearful Thinking 69
Chapter 9   All I Am Not Is All I Am Becoming 76
Chapter 10 Self versus Personal Self 82
Chapter 11 Forgiveness 94
Chapter 12 Joy 103
Chapter 13 Courageous Heart 110
Chapter 14 Companion Tools 119
Chapter 15 Attitudinal Gratitude 135
Chapter 16 Self-Filled Service 151
Chapter 17 Abundant Generosity 166

Questions and Answers 173
Glossary of Terms 183

A MESSAGE FROM THREE ANGELS

In the hollows of what is here now, a whisper is heard.
The echo is almost unperceivable, as if the breath, the one breath,
is traveling to you.

This one breath washes over you, bathing you in warmth,
a golden murmur, and you sigh.

The whirlpool of your thoughts
slows and reconfigures. Some thoughts dissipate; some thoughts crystallize—
and then the exact, premier thought,
your desire, is born.

It offers resolution. The proclamation is
sunshine and daylight.

A hand has been extended to you, and you hesitate, as you should. Focus.
Discern. Choose.
Three wise steps.

The energy of the three speaks in true neutrality. The yes, the no, and the answer.
The black, the white, and the gray. The you, the me, the divine.

The sun is high in the sky. The wind is still.
Another divine song,
sung into who you are.

A hand has been extended to you,
and you hesitate, as you should. Focus. Discern. Choose.
Three wise steps.

The sun drops; the night rises.
A new voice shouts, "Look at me now!" and you realize it is you—
jubilant, enriched,
joyful.

In the dark of the night, the brightest light is seen. It whispers. It echoes. It sings.
It breathes. You sigh.

Down the river you float, at one with
the water, the night, the sun,
the whisper,
the echo, the song,
the one breath.

And then you have the perfectly distilled, premier
thought that heals, and you realize
that the hand extended is your own.

PREFACE

I've been driven many times to my knees by the overwhelming conviction that I have nowhere else to go.
—**Abraham Lincoln**

As morning came, I awoke with the same emptiness. It felt like an unwanted companion, a harsh teacher, or a drill sergeant. My fragile self cried out in desperation. I needed to do something. I moved my body in an attempt to relieve the emotional and mental pain and throw it off a bit so I could get a breath. I knelt on the bed and looked out onto Main Street.

As I scanned the sunlit street, I saw a church. My eyes stopped on the hanging cross in the doorway. *A friend, o rescuer,* I thought. I still did not know what to do as the pain lingered in my throat and chest. I again looked at the cross with tears on my face. With an anguished gasp, I said, "I promise to dedicate my life to serve others if you will rescue me from this hell." I lay down and shut my eyes. I stayed in what felt like a burial position. I crossed my arms over my heart, and my feet were perfectly parallel. My natural mind began to recount the event that had caused my suffering, and my eyes closed tighter as I tried to stop thinking.

That sacred dance of surrender brought on an experience that felt as if I were immersed in a bath of white light. A warm, loving feeling passed through every cell in my body. The spiritual veil was so thin that it changed me forever. I knew it was different, not normal, and not of this world. I felt loved—whole. I felt hugged in a warm embrace that lasted for what felt like an eternity. The lone tear that made its way down my cheek felt cool.

I eventually realized that illumination was a state in which enough barriers of forgetfulness had been divinely dropped that a greater context suddenly presented itself. The experience allowed the inner light of Self to shine through as a profound lovingness. When it was over, I didn't get any messages or visions. I jumped up and started doing push-ups. I put on Supertramp's "Even in the Quietest Moments" and got ready for class. My mind was soft with errant thoughts, but I had just been given a clarity.

I looked out on the same street, but it appeared brighter, illuminated by an internal light. I could describe the residual feeling only as a cushion of love. As I ran past the smiling nun collecting money on Main Street for the poor, I stopped. Without hesitation, I gave her all my food money. She looked at me with a smile, and I ran on, waving my lacrosse stick with a spring in my step. I went right to the chapel and sat down.

From my life-changing revelation, it became clear that my mission in life is to seek that light again and extend it to others who are open to becoming familiar with spiritual principles and disciplines that open awareness and Self-realization. I realized that nothing new is learned; rather, what already exists becomes completely revealed.

I am writing this book for three reasons: to elucidate a way for spiritual seekers to use their life experiences as raw material for spiritual evolution, to provide practical tools for a better life, and to inspire those who are tired of the pain of suffering and dark lessons to pursue their divine right to see the world through the peace inherent in spiritual vision. Undoing truth would be impossible, but spiritual concepts, once learned, practiced, and integrated, will change one's vision.

Once I realized what outdated concepts didn't fit my changing visions, I retrained my eyes, which changed my concept of an outdated self. I was somehow still the same old me, just wiser. I went on to complete my education both as an army mental health technician and as a master's-level social worker. I then worked at a VA hospital in New York for thirty-five years, helping veterans and their families. I raised four children and have a psychotherapy practice focused on the use of spiritual technologies and evidence-based therapeutic interventions. A few examples of these technologies are the practices of humility, gratitude, and surrender. All in all, this book is a manual of options designed to enhance readers' lives by changing their mindset and then their vision by which they see their world. Its tools are accessible for readers ranging from the spiritually curious to those on the path of awakening.

The greatest and most important problems in
life are all in a certain way insoluble. They
can never be solved, only outgrown.
—Carl G. Jung

INTRODUCTION

He who is not busy living is busy dying.
—Bob Dylan

I offer the following spiritual technologies, which I have used formally since my awakening at age twenty, as ways of vision transformation. I have used these tools for the past forty years to bring out my best potential as a person and a healer. After much self-analysis, I found that the personal qualities that emerged were always available as potential on a soul level, behind the veil that separates the seen world from the unseen world. I presently use these practices daily to find peace within myself and become a better being.

My intention was always to become a better healer for others, but the healing of my tendency to live without authenticity and to journey with a natural mind riddled with negative self-talk is happening as well. This negative chatter comes as a derisive partner that, although it can be a call to action for change, often creates suffering. Observing this voice from a distance helped me to heal and correct my dysfunctional, shame-based vision of the world.

We all teach who we are, but the character of some teachers stood out to me. I made it a point to study the holy and kind as I went along, even when I didn't feel worthy or capable of such behavior and often acted as if I was until able to integrate their models into daily practice in the form of the following tools. The use of these tools opened my spiritual heart. The inner change was powerful enough that my vision of myself and the external world was deeply affected. I began to see things through the light behind the veil of the personal self. Once I realized that the work of transformation was unfolding Self, I became curious and excited to find and use a toolbox of tried-and-true mechanisms for change. I then found that the changes could occur slowly or rapidly.

Within a short time, everything I saw and all I did came from a spiritual intention. I began to see the world through spiritual vision. I was no longer fighting to gain fulfillment externally. I saw a world perfectly capable of meeting all my physical, emotional, and spiritual needs. All events, people, and things were suddenly gifts and opportunities to practice love. I realized I was no longer a victim of the natural mind's fear-filled program of inevitability and now had a source of unlimited power at my disposal. I most effectively harnessed this power by using thought technologies.

A technology, as used in this book's context, is a body of knowledge or a spiritual, mental, or physical practice that has the power to change aspects of the seeker's life through changing his or her mindset. These technologies or tools transform normal perception into spiritual vision, which allowed me to go from seeing through my natural mind's limited past experiences and expectations to the divine essence inherent in all people, places, and occurrences. It soon became evident that being spiritual meant seeing lessons and holiness in all things, people, and opportunities that come before and through us. In other words, it is as if we have x-ray vision into the beauty and the meaning behind the social and mundane occurrences in our lives. The spiritual laws of abundance, attraction, and karma can be harnessed through the use of these tools to create the lives we dream of. By keeping our vows and commitments to self and others, we can have the energy to use these tools despite bouts of depression and fear of failure. The tools act as energizers and create a hopefulness that connects to our belief in their power. I only had to choose a tool, such as kindness, and allow its power to work without interference. They worked much like antibiotics. The loving mindsets worked on my shame-based belief system by changing my external perception, and I then realized that wounded personal self was also a story I could heal by objectification and compassion.

    I began to see that I wasn't my natural mind's broken, occluded vision of a victim. I was a unique expression of the divine energies that had always been present in my soul's vortex. I used spiritual tools, such as honesty, vigilance, and compassion, and became better at staying in alignment with Self and making wiser decisions. Please understand that each tool is healing and transformative in itself, and the tools can be used in any order or manner we find most comfortable. We can adjust tools and their usage according to our life circumstances. With open eyes, through spiritual intention, we can watch how opportunities arise to practice any tool we focus on. Another beauty of having options is that we can be creative with the ones we have already integrated into our daily practice. We can use many tools throughout the day, mentally and physically. From my experience, I knew the tools needed to be simple and easy to use, especially under pressure. I could focus on forgiveness as a contemplative idea as a morning prayer and do service for a person in need around lunch. The tools can be utilized mentally or practiced literally in daily prayer, relationships, and crises. I've also found that talking about the tools with others or journaling about them can reinforce their power in our own lives. It soon became evident that I was teaching what I needed to integrate more fully.

These tools also hold a power to energize self-esteem. Each time we successfully practice these technologies and notice their ever-present power to change the moment, we feel good about ourselves. As a result, we can easily choose to extend that good feeling to others. I have always tried to be kind, but once I had simple kindness as a constant companion, I felt safer socially and professionally. My natural mind is often at odds with the purpose of these tools, but through persistence, the natural mind relents for the time being. When I don't use the tools and instead act out of fear, I inevitably experience guilt and shame. I eventually learned to use these two fear-filled helpers to learn not to punish myself. I would go back and study a new tool or reinforce an existing one to avoid the sharp self-awakening system my natural mind set up to help me evolve. As I accepted the natural mind's proclivity to be stubborn and its leanings towards selfishness, I forgave my mistakes quicker and was able to experience more peace sooner. This increased my self-esteem and began to beckon the Self. This Self was always my goal as a spiritual seeker due to its synchronistic qualities and its truly compassionate nature. The Self also exists out of time and reminds us that we are unconditionally loved.

I used some tools for a short period of time, and I used others much longer. Sometimes I would use a tool but soon realize I wasn't able to grasp its meaning at that time. I would often switch to another, at the same time contemplating why the meaning remained hidden. It became a productive search to uproot an existing fear in my belief system. I once tried to forgive a person who had hurt me badly, and I wound up being able to use tolerance. I eventually got to forgiveness but only after learning more from the tool of humility. The practice of these spiritual mindsets allows us to focus our thoughts and emotions and move in a positive direction. Each tool sets the stage for the use of another. They assist each other like teammates on a sports team. My mere intention to use these spiritual mechanisms creates fertile ground for Self-integration and eventual transformation into higher consciousness. This higher vibration is still our unique being, but going forward, it will be referred to as Self. The Self is an aspect of soul that functions without fear and, although still part of the human journey, uses wisdom and compassion to navigate daily. The use of even one tool can be powerful enough to make a visible change in a person's character. It's been my observation that the use of tools is also contagious and fosters communion. Just saying thank you in the vicinity of other people increases the chance they will use gratitude in their practices.

We have a whole arsenal to negotiate what can be a difficult endeavor: life on earth. The use of these tools helps develop positive character, and it can eventually affect our inner and outer life. I have found peace and joy more frequently as well as success at work and at home as a result of their usage. I am most impressed with my social transformation. I now say what I mean, and I rarely say it in a mean way. I look forward to being around others, and I have recently begun to see more beauty in difficult people and situations.

The best part of having this toolbox handy is the safety of reaching for a tried-and-true technology that I don't have to invent. I've felt and seen the power. The tools can empower us in all circumstances to grow as we become conduits of their healing power in the world. I realized I could gauge my success in how deeply integrated the tools were becoming by how frequently and automatically I reached for them. Success was rarely found in a feeling, but I used the tools wisely and with much success. I saw my changes first in the courage, perseverance, and consistency in using the tools. The tools are to be used by the unique individual who chooses to utilize their power in any way needed. They are not mine; they are a gift from love itself. They are to be used creatively.

This book is dedicated to awakening us to the power of spiritual technology. *Spiritual technology* describes thought tools that create readiness for learning and fuel willingness to let go of obstacles that hinder the evolution of our consciousness. The devoted spiritual person journeys with a courageous heart in a dualistic land. To many, this earth school appears confusing and conflictual. If we look at the rules of living on earth, we can clearly see into the core of how contrast clears the fog blocking spiritual truth. We see extremes everywhere and are constantly asked to make choices between them. All these choices have an effect on our lives, and they serve as guides by which to learn.

Duality comes in the form of comparisons and contrasts that allow experiences in life to stand juxtaposed to each other so they may be seen more clearly. We wouldn't know cold without hot, light without dark, or peace without suffering. My teacher once explained how spiritual truth is often hidden best in paradoxical wisdom. Much of this book is a good example of how learning can seem like either a prison house or a road to freedom. You will notice that one aspect of our thinking has no escape and always creates confusion, suffering, and death. This dead end, combined with grace and faith, can be enough to bring curiosity and a deep desire to heal and strive for peace of mind. The earth school, with its specific laws of duality and cause and effect (karma), can bring us up and out of this finite prison if we live with our eyes and ears open to the miracles available in the eternal now of everyday life. Duality, by nature, shows us where we are, and it gives us a map to where we would like to travel. Cause and effect is also a perfect teacher, as it illuminates our path in time so we can choose again and again, so adjustments can be made. The choices we make and their subsequent creations are our lives.

I hope this book serves as a daily manual for spiritual seekers on any path to awaken. This guide helps us create the most vibrant lives available. The path of a modern-day seeker must be tailored to fit his or her busy life and each seeker's capacity and readiness for truth, regardless of the technological interface he or she chooses: ritual, religion, yoga, meditation, or another form of technology designed to facilitate a more vibrant life. I hope something within these pages will be of loving service. To move in vibrant ways on the spiritual path takes a courageous heart. To move in vibrancy, we have to remember that we must embrace the light and dark aspects of life and the personal self equally.

The evolution of natural mind into divine mind of Self is best served once we become clear about what we are seeking. Are we seeking consciousness on a higher plane? Are we seeking peace of mind or health of body? These questions help readers negotiate the following thought tools and identify the ones that fit best. This book is asking readers to take deliberate control of conscious thought and send an invitation to the Self to transform them into peaceful, benevolent people. One must journey with an open heart into the mental and emotional belly of the beast so as to get as much direction as possible. This is the purpose of the two spiritual laws mentioned earlier. Establishing clear goals at least periodically throughout the journey will help reassure us that the trip into Self is worth it.

To begin any journey, especially one of the heart and mind, we must delve deeply into what could be new ground and hold a desire to stay in alignment with Self as a holy character above all else. In this case, *holiness* does not necessarily refer to religious correctness or interfere with any community goal. Instead, *holiness*, as stated earlier, refers to a state of being that I will refer to hereafter as Self. This Self is the dualistic counterpart of the personal self, which is an accumulation of many experiences and attachments that are a combination of our karmic propensities and earth-life programming. The personal self identifies with a separate body in space and time and is run by a level of consciousness designed and often motivated by lack, fear, and victimhood learned in the past. The Self—our actualized, most integrated being—is so awakened that it brings love, wisdom, and invulnerability in any and all circumstances. The Self is a spiritual entity that is not limited to intellect and the dualistic human heart.

For many of us, the power of this soul expression will take on a unique form in our lives and can express itself no matter what our spiritual goals are. This will happen as we allow ourselves to be continually taught by everything on the divine path and move through our fears and naiveties. We can feel the presence of Self in a sunset or a hug, and the more aligned we are with its vortex of vibration, the more we will call it in with direct intention. Spiritual fulfillment is a reachable goal if we remain steadfast in creating the thought changes that allow the Self to appear.

To evolve spiritually, we must enlist many tools that are more powerful than intellect and prior learning. The thought tools in this manual are designed to sow seeds in the natural mind through the intellect, and with the help of the neutral witness mindset, our learning can eventually break through the limited way we see things and allow wisdom to emerge. The divine mind is analogous to our love-based wisdom, which flows from grace through our Self. The divine mind is the all-knowing decision-maker of the Self and is connected to a knowingness the natural mind and its limited intellect lack. If we listen openly, its divine guidance helps us realize that every step taken brings us one step closer to spiritual fulfillment, whether it appears to take us forward or backward. It may also become clearer from this healing thought that everything on the spiritual journey was divinely placed and inspired. Imagine that all occurrences, whether we label them with dualistic words, such as *good* or *bad* or *holy* or *evil*, are somehow perfect for our healing and subsequent soul evolution on earth. Spiritual fulfillment has an opportunity to be felt once we look at life with our eyes and hearts open, knowing that the highest good is always being served with every step. Surrendering is an imperative tool on a path that often feels unfamiliar. The use of this manual and familiarization with the tools and concepts taught will create a fertile ground for walking this journey. The fertile ground for one seeking any goal on the spiritual path is ground of constant alignment with Self and its higher conscious state. Where you place your consciousness is where you awaken. What you look at has life. If you do not see it, it does not exist for you. It only exists outside your perception.

This is a time to do our best to know everything. If you are walking on rough terrain, it will be important to know and be aware of the presence of fertile ground; it is everywhere, and with our eyes and hearts open with the use of meekness, we will see all the lessons with better clarity. This revelation, combined with our dedicated use of the tools prescribed within this manual, can act as the fuel for evolution on earth. Every situation properly perceived becomes an opportunity to heal.

The strength of our commitments and our willingness to let go of what we wish to see will plant peace, love, and wisdom in our lives so we can serve our fellow humans and live in oneness as Self on earth.

I purposely designed the structure and flow of this book to create a relationship with thought tools and the interlocking matrix by which they are expressed. Some tools will resonate more than others, but do not get stuck on a concept judged as too simplistic or too complex. The use and integration of one tool can become the miracle that gives freedom from an obstacle that might be blocking the light of another one. Some materials are repeated in many chapters as a reminder that all the material is essential to the whole. It is my hope that this book and its technology will appear as a lovely rhythm by which we can integrate recurring themes into practical expression in our daily lives. Our commitment to learn consciously through willingness and desire leads to the intake of wisdom. Experience integrates everything into transformative thoughts and fuels the courage and vigilance to use the tools outlined in this book more frequently. The spiritual path works best when we are sincere in our attempts to study and practice daily. Once we are aware that we will run into strong resistance and return to old natural-mind coping skills, we can use the gift of forgiveness to keep moving forward despite feelings of failure and disappointment. The greatest gift we can give ourselves is to stop self-judgment altogether and focus on the usefulness of our choices through awareness. The lack of self-judgment will help the neutral witness to bring more clarity and remove obstacles. This Self perspective will allow the flow of joy to be an ever-present partner on the journey. I am becoming more solid in the belief that despite external circumstances, I am loved beyond my ability to understand.

Part one of the book presents concepts and tools designed to remove any obstacles to living in Self. The core spiritual tools and concepts presented can all be integrated on a daily basis as we navigate our temptations and challenges. Part two will present companion tools and practical advice on how to apply the concepts from part one. There is also a glossary of terms at the end of the book to help give further clarity of terms used and concepts introduced.

In the light of clarity, I see your smiling face, in the dark emptiness, I feel your loving embrace.
—Reverend Corinne Ramage

CHAPTER 1
LISTENING TO LIFE

Every minute of life carries with it miraculous value and it is a face of eternal youth.
—**Albert Camus**

A friend once said that if I opened up a profound book to any passage, it would be the one I needed to read. This set in motion a wonderful pastime, which I extended to others. If the divine is in everything and is everywhere, especially our divine mind, then messages can come in any form and at any time. If we can release all agendas, outcomes, and self-centered goals and not put out into the world only what we want to see, hear, or experience, we can be in communion regularly with divine presence and possibly progress on the path with greater joy and wonder. All social interaction has the capacity to be a teaching device, and each person can illuminate the curriculum for our continued growth. Without the constructs of contrast, comparison, and contemplation, the natural mind will revert to the default of its tried-and-true fear-based tools. People are creative mirrors of the things we need to change or reinforce in our personal self. What if we began to believe with our whole heart that our answers are always being given, and our loving creative source is in constant communion with us? To truly grasp this mind-blowing natural concept, we must at least begin to understand how this belief can illuminate our innate worthiness as it reaffirms our divine heritage over and over again. An important precept that can help make this clearer is to look beyond the mundane happenings of daily life to the abstract. Focusing and meditating not on content but on context gives us this fertile ground.

Ordinary life is never just ordinary. The sacred path starts when we are curious about where the divine resides on a daily basis. This aesthetic intention is the core of the sacredness in our lives and comes from the quintessential and illuminating love at the root of all things and occurrences. This is why any divine message can be seen, heard, and reverenced.

We awaken slowly on earth to the divine Self. The beauty of time is best seen as it allows the divinity unique and newly present in all things to unfold slowly. We can see it over and over and feel love as it plays its intermittent song to the feelings created by fear. Many of us curse time and live impatiently, but if we realize how helpful it is to have multiple chances and choices, we are more grateful. The more we look at our lives on earth as energized and supported by a divine source, no matter its name, the more our perceptions can change to spiritual visions. This belief forms an evolutionary rung on the ladder of consciousness. From this perspective, we can better experience the restoration of the conscious awareness of the inheritance of our wholeness. This occurrence brings clarity by allowing us to see the divinity reflected in all things as we experience them. Once we set our intentions to evolve on a spiritual level, the soul begins to bring forth new abilities already alive in our vortex of Self. The ability to see the blessed synchronicity in nature and in the actions of others energizes our curiosity to learn more and become transformed through the integration of these truths.

This concept takes some getting used to since we are usually focused on the dark end of the dualistic aspect of life's travails. To awaken quicker, we can imagine the earth as a holy school with a great outcome that has the ability to nurture us and help in our daily lessons, no matter what life seems to be showing. What if we embrace and grow into people who strive to receive guidance mainly from divine mind? Will we become more accustomed to its blessings? I envision a time when there is no duality, when all is of equal relevance and is relevant and inconsequential at the same time. There is no learning in nonduality, because learning depends on time. We will be thinking from a source beyond, and in this beyond, everything is known. This place of beyond can be a goal for serious spiritual seekers. Whatever we hold in mind consistently is always a reference point, and as we use the spiritual tools, such as neutral witness, we will be able to see how far we've progressed. Our understanding of the earthly laws of cause and effect and duality can empower automatic surrender of our reliance on the natural mind. Through this fearless perspective, we can see all that happens on earth as a means to soul evolution. This beyond concept requires dedication and faith that can allow the truth to be communicated in all ways and through all things.

My son noticed three crows on the wire above our yard one day. He asked, "What are they saying, Dad?" I immediately went to an animal totem book and looked up the significance of crows. I found out crows were messengers and harbingers of creativity. The following day, my son told his teacher that he was feeling creative and molded a sculpture that I still have twenty years later. That sculpture still inspires me. He still asks me to look up all significant animals he sees in dreams and animals, birds, or insects that stand out to him throughout his day. I love how all things that move and catch our attention in nature can be seen as a constant gift of communication. Imagine seeing all that happens and everything that comes into sight as part of an ongoing communion.

At work one day, some colleagues ran out to tell me there was a family of ladybugs by the window. I counted their spots and explained the nature of grace to those who would listen. We talked about it being a lucky day. I live this truth daily and spend my day in communion, no matter where I am. When I am centered, numbers appear on mailboxes. I look them up in my pocket numerology book. Each number has a message, especially if it comes in a dream or keeps showing up in numerous places. I can't lie and say I haven't played some in the lottery, because I have, and of course, I have yet to win. I guess the message was my winning.

Self also speaks constantly and lovingly through my daily interactions. Even if I miss the messages, they show up again and again. That is what love does, right? It's always saying, "I am here—notice me!" All spiritual tools are helpful because they can act like refresh buttons that clear the clouds of perception and allow clarity to reign. This level of living consciously helps create constant reinforcement of our divine heritage and our holy connection, despite constant trips back into the natural mind for alleged comfort. The more I grew in spiritual confidence, the more it seemed my natural mind felt threatened, and fearfully separated, it attempted to reinforce its fruitless options by putting me in a dark mood and holding the victim card in full view. Feelings are not facts, but they are surely messengers that tell us we are not aligned with Self. I then work to deny my personal ignorance when I am conscious and revel in my connection in every way. In this case, denial is not blindness to the feeling but a way of pushing it away so as to live mindfully once more. My occasional feelings of separation from the divine can also create an increase in the use of all spiritual tools and reinforce my compassion for the plight of humanity as it strives to overcome its apparent state of physical separation.

When I am vigilant and centered, I am even able to hear the lyrics to old songs more clearly. These lyrics are often relevant to what I am going through at that moment. Songs are a perfect way to listen to divine messages, because the vibration is literal and moving. This helps us remember better than mere words do. I listened to the rock group Yes for two years straight, getting all I could from the spiritually inspired lyrics. After thirty years, I realized some of the lyrics were different than I had originally perceived them. They were much deeper. I guess I was not yet ready to receive their depth as a younger person.

This brings up an important issue about levels of preparation. Being ripe for truth also played a part when I read certain books. I arrogantly thought I ingested the wisdom in these masterpieces, but after reading them several times, I found the books contained completely different messages. It was as if a different person were reading the same books. When I was ready to receive the messages, I saw that some lessons come out of sequence. In those times, my spiritual maturity either blocked or deferred the truths conveyed. I also became aware that living in a material world can preoccupy and insulate us from change and growth because of the amount of responsibility that distracts us.

For the soul, human life is all good. It is truly for us to live in joy and love, despite what appears on the news or in our neighborhoods, by realizing love is inside and around us constantly if we persist in looking, listening, and opening our hearts. A wonderful friend told me that prayer was useful to her because of its clearing effect. She used prayer as a centering tool so she could be more aware of the holiness in her mundane life. She connected to the infinite source of the earth by walking without shoes as often as possible on grass or the beach to release all heavy and challenging things. She felt transformed by walking on the beach, rolling in the grass, and looking at the sky at night. Releasing all things to spirit brought wonderful lessons into the wake of what was released. She lived with both feet in this world, and she surrendered all conflicting energy into the creative energy source of nature.

Energy is never lost; it is just transformed. Many seekers who do yoga and meditate know how to release negative energy through the vessel of the body, which brings good physical and spiritual health. Negative energy occurs as we hold on to fear-filled thoughts, which can eventually become resentments and vengeful mindsets. The earth constantly calls us to breathe in its gifts and breathe out that which does not serve us. As we release that which does not serve us into the earth, we receive what helps us grow and maintain an inner light. We are of the earth, learning through duality and cause and effect.

We often do not know what we need until we lose it. This is the way of the earth; it is how the earth teaches. In loss or the absence of inner peace, we realize what we need. The sacredness on earth can help us evolve with more peace if we maintain centered and clear minds and strive constantly to have open eyes and ears in an intention to evolve. We can see and recognize needed information in what is painful or fulfilling. The sacred is speaking in your life but might not be visible. We always have a choice to integrate either pain or peace and connect with faith to an infinite source. Many find that once they become more comfortable with meditation and contemplation, they learn valuable lessons more quickly and with less suffering.

If these practices aren't comfortable, try to find some deep quiet or stillness. These tools help us decipher the daily messages. I often get counsel from my teachers and like-minded friends in conversation to get other takes on messages or dreams. Use everything available since your devotion fuels the quest to hear your beloved source communicate daily and nightly. A big clue to staying conscious as we keep vigilant for divine messages is the use and control of guilt and shame. When these two natural-mind default mechanisms become dominant parts of personal-self scripts and rule the mind, they block divine messages. I eventually learned they are not to be obliterated. Some spiritual seekers believe the repression of these tools is the measure of success in holiness. In reality, a full understanding of their lessons leads to a vibrant spiritual life. Guilt and shame are dark divine teachers if used in the conscious mind. These emotional states keep your life on track in specific situations. If they dominate morning to night, they must be resolved and integrated. I used truth and prayer with their handling and, at times, good counsel from loving others.

The following are a couple of the most precious truths: (1) no journey is incomplete, and (2) all journeys are revered and all souls are incarnate for the continuation of specific spiritual missions. This book proposes that the earth is a benevolent school in which only love exists, despite appearances. Spiritual vision opens up the ability to see how all occurrences, even ones deemed sad, dark, and cruel, play a part in our perfect awakening on many levels. How can we know that dark lessons aren't exactly what is called for at that time to evolve? All information that breaks through perception, especially revelatory understanding and spiritual truth, is a form of creation. All that occurs or shows itself can be considered like food to the digestive system. Digesting food is unconscious; digesting knowledge is intentional and creates personal growth. Digesting spiritual truths creates enlightenment.

Many seekers love learning through reading or wise teachers. It serves them and should be utilized until they are ready to get the egg directly from the hen by hearing the powerful whisper of Self. We all have our own unique spiritual wisdom, and living consciously brings a wonderful uncovering as we progress. Self-revelatory thoughts are the transformational movements that change everything, but they cannot be touched if spiritual digestion is not accomplished. Digestion makes spiritual evolution personal. Spiritual seekers must delve deeply into their journeys and travel with trust. It can be frightening to go where an individual human seeker has not gone before. The trips back and forth into the natural mind and through our mistakes can be used as weapons that fight the status quo and become blessed learning opportunities. We must be able to return to the familiar or risk giving up at crucial times. With much devotion, we can and will eventually begin to know the truths we were not ready to handle in the beginning of the journey toward peace.

Autobiography in Five Chapters
Portia Nelson

I. I walk down the street. There is a deep hole in the sidewalk. I fall in. I am lost … I am helpless. It isn't my fault. It takes me forever to find a way out.

II. I walk down the same street. There is a deep hole in the side-walk. I pretend I don't see it. I fall in again. I can't believe I am in the same place, but it isn't my fault. It still takes a long time to get out.

III. I walk down the same street. There is a deep hole in the sidewalk. I see it is still there. I still fall in … it's a habit. I know where I am. It's my fault. It still takes a long time to get out.

IV. I walk down the same street. There is a deep hole in the side walk. I walk around it.

V. I walk down another street.

CHAPTER 2
NEUTRAL WITNESS

We are all serving a life sentence in the dungeon of self.
—**Cyril Connolly**

Spiritual seekers who incorporate spiritual tools every day to increase conscious awareness may find their curiosity piqued for additional ways to ignite the spirit and empower the search. This spiritual intention is a high calling that naturally moves people in unexpected ways. Living a vibrant life is a combination of extremes; it is a blending of conflicting earth lessons and movements of the soul in our daily lives. Navigating these power-filled lessons and movements calls for tools and technologies that give strength and clarity. Soul lessons often go unnoticed, but they appear in both light and dark occurrences. For instance, they could be about tolerance or compassion, but both can lead to revelations that help connect us to healing. Curiosity is eventually replaced by staying conscious, surrendering any obstacles that block our progress, and staying the course. Curiosity can create a willingness to go into our shadow self, which has an empowering effect on all we do on the path to awakening. This shadow is all the negative aspects of the personality that are motivated by fear.

The neutral witness is a tremendously powerful state that can be considered a foundation of spiritual evolution technology. This tool goes by many names and is reached for in many practices and on many paths. Some call it the observer or the inventory taker, and it is behind the use of meditation in many cultures. It is generally agreed that intended focus is imperative for progressing consciously as people or as spiritual seekers. The willingness to access a neutral space and observe what goes on in the natural mind acts as a door for divine wisdom and is imperative if we are to sort through beliefs and limiting or self-destructive thought streams.

The spiritually-minded seek to transcend the body and intellectual mind altogether. Neutrality acts as a two-way lens that can be envisioned as a place between the natural mind and the higher mind that can reinforce the curiosity created from learning or suffering. This positive practice gives us a place to observe, discern, and allow. It can also create a distance that uncovers more opportunities to choose positive practice choices, such as tolerance, acceptance, and forgiveness, as we navigate the divinely inspired lives we walk. The neutral witness helps us observe and bypass past programming and agendas to see messages in both dark and light. This is helpful as we look for truth and love, since they hide in our limited perceptions. The conscious use of light and dark gives us the ability to understand lessons as we walk through our days. The contrasts they create give maximum clarity, despite our emotions. The neutral witness is a higher-mind tool that exists out of time. It can observe past and present in a wondrous light. The higher mind consists of the thoughts generated by Self. This aspect of mind is a voice of wisdom and unconditionality that, although subtle, can become a primary guide for all choices.

When we become sharply awakened to lessons learned through physical pain or pleasure or emotional comfort or discomfort, we still have to process clues. As they are integrated into daily life through thought, transformation can occur. It is harder when we try to decipher lessons from the emotional part of our lives, because of their diversity and conflict-ridden distance. Any deeper learning can be more easily ascertained through right-minded thinking or higher mind. When we look at any lesson without all the emotional energy generated by longing for the past or misperceptions about the past, clarity comes more easily. As I will discuss later, it doesn't always serve us to have only light lessons, given the nature of perception to cover up pain and suffering and minimize their blessings. The tool of neutrality serves as a gate to a beyond that brings the inner voice into alignment with wisdom. A meaningful use of Self-evolving wisdom is the learning and practice of anything that helps us to focus and change beliefs that block the awareness of our innate divinity. We can proceed with confidence when we use spiritual technology to awaken, and an increase in inner peace is the sign we are aligned with our soul mission, no matter how diverse or unknown to us it is at the time. The daily use of the neutral mind space often increases the willingness and faith in its future use. Human choices also yield better results, and our level of spiritual vision grows. Spiritual vision is a way of seeing meaning and lessons in all that comes before us in our daily lives.

Observing any dysfunction or misalignment in neutrality accelerates movement away from dysfunction and accelerates healing. When we move to neutrality to get clarity, we are more in the flow of divine time as its pace slows for a better look. To move to the deep silence of this mindset, we can use many practices. Many people use forms of centering practices initiated and maintained by deep, cleansing breaths. Some use mudra hand gestures or sacred phrases, such as *om* or *Abba*. It is important to note that it is not the practice that returns one's attention to the healing space; it is the intention to return. This allows for the possibilities of more faith, patience, and wisdom to join us. In general, neutrality helps us grow a seamless relationship to all experiences, and it brings to light the divine underbelly of what lies within. As dedicated spiritual seekers, we are constantly asked to observe without the judgment of good and bad and move beyond to an initial lens that involves either fear or love. Through the use of humility and spiritual contemplation, one can feel and see the positive fruits and mistakes of past choices and use these understandings to rely on a wisdom that is increasingly accessed through the use of the neutral witness. This observation system also allows us to use the natural mind to set and reach finite goals until they are no longer needed to journey.

One of the biggest obstacles a spiritual seeker can encounter is a lack of ability and confidence in being able to discern the impulsive thinking of natural body-mind and the divine voice of Self. The Self's subtle whisper easily gets overpowered by the shouting and impatient voice of the self. With the neutral witness in place, one can see and hear better in order to discern if the fearful self or the love-filled Self is communicating and when it is communicating. This allows for patience and the oneness alluded to in many spiritual and scriptural writings. In this oneness, listening comes without effort. In the sacred space of neutrality, we can allow things to pass us by that could derail or detour peace. This marriage of body-mind concerns and divine-mind knowingness becomes one and works more practically in our daily lives. We watch, in a way, from above the battlefield. The neutral witness allows us to take constant inventory of our belief structures as they evolve, shed, or update positions that no longer apply. There are always higher and more inclusive compassionate truths that can be brought forth. The truth on earth for dedicated spiritual seekers is variable and constantly evolves, and it is at the mercy of a faulty device called perception. Perception has a limiting tendency to see only what it is looking for. We must stay open to guidance and remain awake in humble learning. The truths we believed and needed to hold at different stages on the path of the evolution of our consciousness might no longer be appropriate or resonate as love.

The world of dualistic learning allows for extreme experiences and extreme teachers. As discussed earlier, pain is as powerful a teacher as love, but they do not feel the same. Every choice on earth seems to have a consequence, good or bad, given our limited ability to understand the divine mind. This is often caused by our resistance to having faith in a future or process we're not yet sure of. We often default to feeling victimized by something or someone. Choices made impulsively and without discernment can make our lives seem confusing and fearful. In a state of neutrality, we can use witnesses to play any tape. We can rewind old tapes for lessons, watch old lessons again, or fast-forward to future choices to avoid certain consequences. We would be better off remembering that all lessons are soul expressions on the sacred journey. They are brought to attention only to be healed and to teach, not to victimize, as the body-mind would have us believe.

When we feel overwhelmed, we can be pulled into acting impulsively in ways that are not sorted out through neutrality. When we rely on perception and impulse, we run the risk of creating choices that have consequences that have to be undone for resolution. Mistakes are a big part of the learning process on earth. No matter how hard we try to be perfect, there is no way out of this inevitable trial-and-error system since we have a natural mind limited by fear and a perception hindered by its need for constant self-assurance. The tools practiced in neutrality allow for learning that builds higher self-love and compassion as we navigate our lives. All choices and temptations are opportunities for learning. We are never doing anything wrong. Some choices might be less fruitful, and the series of events or outcomes set forth by these less fruitful choices might require some undoing. More destructive choices might have more to undo, but the soul is eternally innocent.

Our spiritual laws on earth, although apparently unseen, are based on the physical laws. For example, cause and effect can be called the law of action and reaction. In another sense, we are all bound by both physical and spiritual laws, which all influence the mental, emotional, and spiritual aspects of the search for Self. The soul serves as a spiritual bank account. It stores our learning and helps create lessons that are especially designed for awakening. If we do not heal a lingering resentment toward another, it can hold the natural mind hostage and can then create suffering through the consequence of what is perceived as a dark teacher with painful lessons. This pain-induced learning builds pressure and can create confusion and hopelessness, which can cause us to use outdated coping strategies.

Even though going backward can be uncomfortable, it is part of the dualistic learning experience. It helps in the creation of courageous hearts. The prompt use of the neutral witness tool offers us distance from what is going on in our lives. It sheds light on the lessons that hide in the dark as we stand back and choose from a place of wisdom. It helps us unwrap the lessons, navigate around dark teachers, and avoid suffering. We can intend to learn only by light lessons of love and intellectual learning, but that approach might not serve us best. When we incorporate surrender, we allow the present teacher to do its best work.

The use of spiritual technology in general opens the door to the sacred heart. This vibrationally higher aspect of Self fully and completely accepts all that occurs in our lives as divinely inspired by love while retaining an individual mindset based on personal experience. As we become more familiar with the higher mind and its whisper of higher-vibration truths, we might eventually be able to hold an attitude of gratitude for the dark lessons and teachers and practice levels of forgiveness that change our limited perception and perspectives to spiritual vision. Once one becomes more certain on the path of surrender and more familiar in the previously unfamiliar mindset of the neutral witness's neutrality, one can choose to enter them quickly and frequently. As in other spiritual endeavors, a curious stirring gives way to certain movements into mastery. In the beginning of a relationship with neutrality, one might even be able to access a still place that feels appealing. The part of neutrality that is a still point can be a place of peace while one observes the battlefield of dualistic learning from above. The still point can also serve as a reminder to return often.

In summary, the neutral witness is a mindset that brings on a stance of true neutrality as a thought technology one can access best through the practice of surrender. Once we become more familiar and versed in the nonjudgmental tolerance found in this divine tool, we can develop advanced clarity and confidence of vision that can help us observe and bypass obstacles to our awakening. This practice can also serve to create the best possible life on earth. This ability to be fully spiritually present on the earth and access the divine mind of Self reinforces my belief that our innate divinity comes from our inheritance as a soul. Grace, peace, joy, and invulnerability are our rewards for the persistence and courage it takes to live as spiritual beings in such a challenging realm. Through the practices of meditation and contemplation, we see the mind as a vessel with many rooms. The ultimate goal is to access this neutral room as a tool when it is needed most.

Try the following exercise, which might be helpful in further understanding this tool: Picture yourself in a huge room with two windows facing each other and a comfy chair right in the middle. You are in the chair. Thoughts, feelings, and experiences come in one window and come by you with total clarity. In the clarity of neutrality, you choose which of these are truly helpful to your journey to peace. The rest are allowed to pass and travel out the adjacent window. In this practice, choices help you create a life that can be used as a gift for the world. Peace and the Self are accessible on the other end of the threshold of this sacred door. This portal is held open by the heart of the neutral witness state of mind.

CHAPTER 3
SACRED JOURNEY

Awareness is therapy per se.
—**Fritz Perls, MD**

Spiritual fulfillment is attained in surrendering to live with eyes and hearts open, knowing that the highest good is served with each step taken. No matter how far you look back or project forward, life is holy in the mind of Self. Our life occurrences are often shrouded by drama, but they are always the raw material for awakening. If we journey with faith and a belief that we are loved unconditionally by the divine rather than wandering in fear of impending punishment, we can better tolerate feelings of inevitability and overcome the limited beliefs the natural mind uses to keep the body safe. The belief that we are of divine inheritance helps us strive more fearlessly toward any spiritual goal. For most, these goals are unconscious, but they are accessible with effort. Imagine that our every step, whether in a backward or forward direction, is blessed and inspired. We must continually trust, whether our lives are spiraling out of control or meeting our needs in ways hoped for, that both directions are one in meaningful purpose.

To understand this better, we must remember that the ability to see clearly what is of divine origin is usually occluded. We see with a pair of eyes limited by their need to reference the past and project their own agenda; thus, we barely have a clue when truth is being spoken in the eternal now. We often attempt to discover who we are in what we think we should be or what others think we should be. We move in a world of shadows, going back and forth between grace and obscurity. The good news is that these extremes of light and darkness trigger experiences that energize us to grow and evolve in ways we might not have consciously planned. The natural mind is always looking for experiences and relationships to define itself through contrast. This compare-and-contrast approach often helps us feel rewarded, remembered, and recognized. These primitive feedback loops are exactly what is needed on the level of personality as the natural mind strives for self-definition. The personal self can then be seen and understood with greater clarity in the light of someone or something other than our self-centered reference point. We can then observe every accomplishment or failure in order to judge our place in a predesigned value system. This system attempts to trigger a fleeting feeling of fulfillment and satisfy the natural mind's striving for pleasure.

The persona uses many vantage points (persons, objects, and experiences) to develop and know who it is as an separate individual. That's why relationships, whether dark or light, are sacred, and when seen through spiritual tools, such as gratitude, they are powerful helpers in our attempt to define our limited personal nature. Perception acts as a constantly changing mirror of personal self with its repetitious, ever-changing character traits. When we glimpse and grasp to feel an anchor, we come away with a transient story of a persona that grows, shrinks, and invariably changes as who we are perpetually ebbs and flows. The personal self appears to live at the mercy of the shifting sands of physical reality and the conditionally based relationships that make up our lives. Once we grow more accustomed to using spiritual vision, we can see that this self acts like a stunt double for soul experiences as it strives to keep both our spiritual promises and our search for fulfillment as a person.

The search for self-fulfillment is perfect. Its limited experiences bring vibrancy and curiosity for something beyond. In a journey that is deeply devoted to uncovering Self, we will eventually be challenged to discard the accumulated patchwork self held in the natural mind. This self gets addicted to drama and possibly negative behavior as it searches mostly in the dark. This searching can create the type of longing only suffering can bring, and in that pain, some rededicate their lives to the search for peace. Many are mired in the status quo and get lost in distractions and habits that create more suffering. Even this practice can precipitate the willingness and spurious movement through mistakes. The mastery of this dark path can serve spiritual evolution by bringing forth a heightened compassion and energized courage. In the uncovering of Self, infinite abilities unfold as more and more aspects of the soul's vortex of potentialities emerge from their patient hiding places, seeking resolution and harmony.

This personal self we identify through attachment to a separate body in space and time has a story that we might not like. What if our endeavors in an experiential world of change and resistance are leading us to the humble realization that nothing in the world is ours or worth keeping? At this point of fertile awareness, we can choose to delve deeper into the sacred journey, spurred on by the stirrings of curiosity and fueled by a renewed courage. It can be frightening to travel where you have never been and do so with trust. To remedy this, we must loosen our expectations for how the journey should look and relinquish as much preexisting judgment as possible. The natural mind habitually evaluates spiritual experience through an outdated self-evaluation system called *the past* as it tries to judge new experiences. When using this outdated and limited comparison system, we must be mindful of self-forgiveness in an effort to quell the bubbling up of fear stored in a body of pain living in the unconscious. On the sacred journey, we will be reminded often that although the two selves appear to conflict, they are actually creating a path perfectly designed to bring forth only Self as our main level of consciousness with more clarity, no matter which way we travel.

Since we are always at the mercy of the law of duality, we often go back to old self-coping styles, such as manipulation, denial, bullying, ritual, and other rigid patterns from the past. This can actually become a gift that allows us to heal at the deepest levels. These skills are primitive and only serve to reinforce the suffering caused by fear and lack unless we allow for their integration. Once this is done, we might see a Self emerging out of the balance of our dark and light aspects. This Self has a vision of life that is less attached to strivings and desire and more aligned with acceptance and tolerance. Even as we work devotedly and strive to evolve, we might occasionally regress and use fear-based coping skills again in certain situations. When our consciousness has progressed enough that we react only from a divine mindset, old coping skills are no longer necessary. Until then, we might find ourselves defenseless in a challenge or temptation and need to regress as a means to rebalance. Old coping mechanisms also serve in duality to help clarify effectiveness. Without the knowledge that we can return to the familiar, we might abandon the spiritual journey or compromise its meaningfulness, leaving ourselves misaligned and without the wisdom we crave.

What are our spiritual goals? This question should be constantly revisited. Spiritual seekers will be constantly asked to choose to become the purest, most authentic expression of love possible, but all will choose what is needed for fulfillment in the present. The sacred underbelly of truth lies in all journeys, no matter how light or dark, obscured or clear. This sacredness is seen in an increase of our devotion, which can take us on countless paths, even ones we label as evil or mediocre. Every soul expression is divinely held and supported. Knowing this can help our integration and transformation if we keep our eyes open to the divinity within each opportunity. Spiritual devotees in the past usually reached for heaven in any way they believed meaningful. This book proposes that mistakes are perfect in their ability to teach and awaken and that our true nature is of an impenetrable, heavenly innocence. Utilizing a forgiveness mind can help remove the preprogrammed obstacles of judgment and attack to allow us to acquire the knowledge needed to live vibrantly. To handle the belief in sin, we must confess and own transgressions or regressions as we move to the more fertile ground of forgiveness. *Sin* is a label for ignorance and the mistakes that ensue.

We are best served when we accept that the natural mind can live in constant attack and self-judgments, and without the use of forgiveness, we might live in a hellish thought loop of unresolved mistakes. In truth, mistakes aren't mistakes; they are just products of limited sight. If we accept that concept, we can move past the wreckage of what no longer exists and go about undoing what was poorly chosen. The practices of self-forgiveness and acceptance enable us to feel the power of all lessons. In hindsight, we often realize the action we took was the best we could have done at that time. As we change our beliefs and surrender, the journey unfolds. We might not understand our answers right away and might be forced to patiently await their wisdom at a later time. This wisdom can often arrive in the form of a future revelation after more learning or traumatic experiences have taken place. Since we're used to our natural minds being full of fear, we often perceive what unfolds through the lens of fear and await our punishments.

I hope the concepts espoused in this book are analogous to building a ladder out of this pain. Each technology serves as a rung to allow for a higher consciousness to empower choices. These choices increase joy and can make us carriers of the technology to others.

In this new sacred thought model espousing that all is good, there is no punishment, because there's never a victim, only a teacher or student. Only love shows us the way to our lessons. Each choice attracts these lessons, and through cause and effect and duality, we have a chance to learn. This type of journey into the heart of light and dark might bring us deeper into conflict, but with the help of spiritual technology, we can grow and gain revelations as we integrate and transform. Each time we use a tool from the spiritual toolbox, we put a rung on the ladder of consciousness. As we climb higher, we move more firmly into the sacred heart of grace and toward personal fulfillment.

One of the positive results of seeing life as a sacred journey into the Self is the growing feeling of power and certainty. Our spiritual eyes don't see fault or sin; they see mistakes. Mistakes can be forgiven, and in this model of evolution, all are innocent and naive, no matter what their earthly journey appears to be. Through a mind built on the structure of compassion, we can even prevent problems in the future. Without the need to repress the pain of guilt and shame, we clearly see our divine lesson presented in a welcoming light. This growing familiarity with innocence allows us to stop evaluating spiritual gains and losses. We can realize how limited and faulty our self-judgment systems really are when we see them from neutral standpoints. What if perceived gains were really consolatory regressions? What if loss was really the breaking of meaningless habits? How can we evaluate the gains and losses?

It often seemed many people in my life appeared unmovable in resistance or lacking in effort until they became heroes in transformation. When we end up surrendering to trust and letting go of controlling outcomes, an influx of grace, with its illuminating wisdom, can light the way. There is no wrong way to interpret lives' happenstance. Some ways are enriching, and other ways are less so. Life itself becomes the teacher as we journey in this purgatorial realm. Purgatory in this sense highlights the constant dance between peace and conflict. This dualistic conflict then becomes the fuel for us to strive to awaken. As we become more aware of being spiritually guided, we gain more confidence in the process of our own evolution. It is even more appealing if we can see the journey as one that has guaranteed a good ending. We are already holy on the only level that's real: the soul. When we begin to feel the presence of sacred love, we realize it is not the version of conditional love we usually see in most of our relationships.

The following thought sequence is handy as a reminder to allow life to unfold on its terms with faith in its loving purpose: You cannot find what you do not know in what you do know. Surrender to what you do not know. Intend to let go of all you know—all the knowledge, all the structure, and all the earthly belief systems that define your present earth-plane reality. Feel what you know dropping away from you. Surrender to the unknown. Free-fall into what is. Surrender with the intention of letting the divine guide you. Surrender, and receive what is from a place of open listening.

Every day the soul sets out to accomplish its mission. No matter if it appears fulfilled or not, it is always complete in its intention to do so. Most people journey unaware that they are walking a beautiful, sacred path. The spiritual seekers have the best chance of perceiving the joy along the way. Because our minds are a blessed fertile ground, every struggle and every success along the sacred path is grist for the mill for our evolution on a soul level.

Focus on the journey, not the destination. Joy is found not in finishing an activity but in doing it.
—Greg Anderson

CHAPTER 4
DUALITY

He who comprehends the darkness in himself, to him the light is near.
—**Carl G. Jung,** The Red Book

If the goal of spiritual evolution is to let go of the meaningless, we must first learn what is meaningful. Duality is the perfect mechanism to teach us what we are not and what we really are as divine beings. This teacher is both a human helper and a doorway to spirit. In the journey to peace, we are given the gift of free will to release the choice for conflict and allow peace's presence. When we choose anything other than peace, we are choosing conflict.

In looking at the importance of understanding duality and its value to spiritual evolution, we must first embrace the fact that the natural mind can only know something by contrast, comparison, or remembrance. These finite tools call for a mechanism that facilitates clarity; once we are clear on something, we can move beyond, allow, and, ultimately, let go of what's not valuable. Duality is also a divine mechanism of clarity in a land that has many hidden teachings and obscure lessons. One must constantly consider the possibility that by using spiritual vision, there is no good or bad. There is only the meaningful or its absence. The limitation of a man-made personal self stirs the curiosity and desire that can channel the energy needed to strive for spiritual evolution. When we tire of fruitless strivings for fulfillment, we might realize that suffering and conflict no longer serve us. We may then develop a desire for a beyond state. This state pulls us into higher levels of consciousness, bringing a better quality of life.

A major theme in a dualistic learning environment is the fruitless repeating of mistakes. This can clearly define the valueless illusions we live by. Once we become tired of repeating meaningless and futile behaviors and using old tools, such as self-reproach and blame, we can begin to integrate new behaviors that render better outcomes. The light-infused technologies espoused in this book, with their positive outcomes, are in direct contrast to the lessons of dark teachers and their suffering and need for undoing and forgiveness. It is true, however, that the repetition of old lessons can be a source of strength, fostering the willingness and humility to deeply surrender. If healing is to occur, we must pay attention to these lessons without judgment and with humility and open-mindedness. Once these tools are in place, we can eventually realize they might help in showing us the best route to any goal. Certain practices, such as contemplation, can enhance the clarity found in duality, especially when enhanced by a teacher's guidance or a designed reading. Ultimately, the familiarization and acceptance of duality as a benevolent teacher and helper minimize the natural mind's tendency to see through the victim's default lens. Without understanding that life works for us through the use of devotion to truth and the steadfast use of spiritual tools, we might become confused and believe that life works against us.

Faith that has no doubt is dead faith. A challenge often encountered by spiritual seekers arises once they start looking for lessons in worldly interactions and relationships. The intellect can block helpful information in a haze of denial and move into the state of a status quo life. Newness is in contrast to the laissez-faire use of the past. It is then easy to accept white lies, poor discipline, or slight resentments without keeping mindful vigilance. The ability to recognize and accept the teachings in duality gives us the best chance to balance our human nature. This equilibrium is the doorway out of the constant push and pull found in resistance and defense that keeps our natural mind and human nature in place as the definers of our lives.

This can lead us back to the incorporation of the neutral witness as a major tool in evolution. Under the canopy of its vision of true neutrality, finiteness and infiniteness are equally important experiences, but they are not equal. Finiteness is about time, process, measurable growth, separation, boundaries, goals, achievements, and completion. All those things have endings. Infiniteness is about soul awakening, resonance, unity, expansiveness, and oneness, which live in the eternal realm. The beauty of finite existence is seen in its ability to call forth the desire to expand and balance. To complete any growth-filled project or heal any miscreation, we need to balance finiteness by observing its consequence in any way accessible at the time and learn its infinite truth.

All possibilities to be explored are already present in duality, and correction and truth are available to be integrated as transformation occurs. We must let go of the belief that light and dark are polar opposites if we are to move beyond. They are, and they are not. Once we come to understand that there is no escape from the rules of duality and stop perceiving the movement of light and dark as journeys in opposite directions, we can balance all experiences. This balance offers the constant option to view all interaction from above the battlefield and clearly be open to what is in front of us. Our ability to learn is greatly enhanced by our acceptance of dark lessons. For most of us, lessons of love are easily accepted, but to a natural mind whose job is to avoid pain, it is difficult to stand tall in darkness and still be a happy learner. A spiritual seeker is often asked to reframe his or her view of life from the perspective of Self and practice seeing the hidden teaching in all occurrences. He or she must do so often without any visible evidence that this change will be helpful.

Balance is powerful when used to handle dualistic lessons, but it takes much vigilance not to choose one extreme over another. To hide in the darkest dark or brightest light is tremendously limiting, as we are often taken out of our comfort zones. Even though it seems more appealing to stay in light and deny dark lessons in life and self, devoted seekers constantly move into unfamiliar territory with courage. In my experience, this is where faith and the belief in a Self that knows the way to peace come in handy. We can move forward in darkness with confidence that we will be successful and experience the power of this mental state of attraction as another tool on the journey. The power of the law of attraction will give the confidence only experienced when one has a belief in Self surety. The more balanced we become in true neutrality, the more wisdom can be accessed from both the natural mind and the divine mind of Self. The belief that the journey of good or light is more desirable because of its pleasurable outcomes stems from the human need for measurement and self-evaluation. When looking for a valuable version of the personal self, victories are more welcomed than defeats. The spiritual journey on earth, once it is understood through cause and effect, is not resisted. This is just another way of saying it leads to the same destination without the need to value the personal self as nothing other than a helper in the process of communication and personal fulfillment on earth. The destination looks and feels different for everyone, but ultimately, it is a destination of evolution and happiness. In the end, balance and duality lead to a beyond where there is no more trial, grace, conflict, or love. There is only a glorious blending of it all. On earth, we are bound to a natural mind that can only use references and contrast to understand concepts. Duality helps us get clarity of what feels pleasurable or painful. Spiritual seekers use this device as a road map to peace.

How do we travel in two directions simultaneously? We can answer this question when we become versed in predominantly seeing from the neutral witness lens. This place is not a gray area or a dilution of light and dark. To see it, we must imagine a gray that is a combination and vibrancy of the brightest light and deepest dark—and then we can only come close.

In conclusion of this all-important chapter about spiritual evolution through duality, we must realize that if we keep on a spiritual trajectory, we are destined to serve as integrated versions of what is here now in complete harmony and total acceptance with all that is. Duality is the ultimate reference guide and measurement tool. In this model, love is actually defined by no love, or indifference, not hate, although it sometimes feels like hate, sadness, or unhappiness. None of these are comparisons, just love's absence. In the quest to spiritually evolve on earth, there is nothing to conquer, because there is no enemy. Happiness is defined by sadness, and the self brings on the Self. It is important to realize that duality is the only way the natural mind learns as it constantly references other people, occasions, and things. As we move toward becoming more familiar with constantly seeing through neutrality, we no longer need extreme opposites to understand who we are and which way to go. We will rarely find ourselves seeking the opposite side of the coin. In true neutrality, opposites come to meet each other. When the yes and no are one, the road is easily traveled into the heart of Self, and others become sacred. The goal on earth varies, but when we use our experiences to measure our intentions and let go of the outcomes, the journey stays fresh. Through faith, even faith that carries doubt, the quality of our lives can be enhanced. Clarity always allows better choices. Choices are the fuel for all movement, both regressive and revelatory. Because of the healing power of duality and the fact that there is no escape from its laws, we can be saved from the natural mind's limitations.

> Befriend your fears. They are you.
> To fight them is to fracture yourself. The harder
> you fight the stronger your fear becomes.
> —Reverend Corinne Ramage

CHAPTER 5
SURRENDER

We cannot change anything unless we accept it first.
—**Helen Keller,** *Memoirs*

Every morning is an important portal for a spiritual seeker. This first awakening is when self-discipline can begin the search for the neutral vantage point that allows for the clear observation of the mindset in which we awoke. When we anchor in the safe house of deep stillness, we can discern between fearful mind and loving mind. We can then begin to align and center on divine and loving mind for our day and walk about more consciously. This practice is akin to making our bed in the morning. This initial step helps us regain the power to make the most enlightened choices. The loving and divine mind of Self always provides unrivaled, pure inspiration. This mind is new, and it is not tethered to past programming or the agenda of the natural mind, which automatically tries to undo the past through obsession or searches for pleasure as it works to stave off past pain. The loving mind moves in the divine flow of grace in the now.

Each morning, if we intend to feel balanced and fulfilled before stepping out into the world, we will be more awake in our lessons. Once we realize that we cannot always get what we need from the world or normal perceptions, curiosity and courage can move us forward into all our endeavors and relationships with a mind wherein divine helpers and wisdom beyond our normal thinking are available to assist. This assistance can be accessed through prayer, service, meditation, or the sacred practice of surrender. What each seeker chooses to surrender—and to whom and how—is unique. Some might allow a divine being to assist or just surrender the burden of a problem or endeavor by giving up control emotionally, mentally, or spiritually. Many have relationships with certain divine masters or deceased relatives whom they feel particularly close to. There is a sacred time in the morning as we wake and in the evening as we lie down to sleep when the spiritual veil is thin. I have always found this an optimum time to become conscious, bring the mind under control, and access wisdom.

The natural mind speaks first as it attempts to get its feet planted on ground that can shift. This uncertainty thus gives impulsive counsel as it lives its fear-based agenda. Much of this fear is fueled by a reservoir of stored guilt and resentment, whether conscious or unconscious, to get us to react. This beautiful, dualistic helper on the human journey lives from the past and always works to resolve unfinished issues to quell pain. Our vigilance and continued inventory of these natural tendencies serve us, as this discomfort constantly reminds us to move beyond its limits in an attempt to live in the eternal now found in the deep stillness of Self. The ultimate goal of many seekers is to become a conduit of divinity on earth.

As we awaken our Self by using the technologies in this book and other spiritual texts and pathways, we move closer to being able to access spiritual and personal potentialities. As we gain more confidence in the tools, such as surrender, our relationship with the personal self and the Self becomes clearer through struggles, trials, and temptation. As this occurs, it opens the dualistic door to allow for the Self to enter as our primary navigation system. We can access all we are and ever will be through acquiring and living on the preexisting eternal level of our innate divinity. The Self brings all its power from its divine source, not the outside world tethered by our limited perception skills. It eventually becomes evident that life-altering revelations are contained within our daily lives, like Easter eggs hidden in the yard. Once we realize this, our consciousness can bring inherent wisdom to light. This aspect of innocent and natural being brings confidence to the daunting journey into new spiritual territory. When we live with trust in the belief of Self, we can access a higher consciousness, which has knowledge our mind has yet to bring forth. To surrender, we must drop the existing tools, beliefs, and defenses we use to navigate in a world we only see in obscurity through perception. In our doing so, it becomes evident that the natural mind is often in conflict with Self. This is a direct consequence of how the flimsy structure of perception is incapable of giving the certainty inherent in divine mind.

The tool of surrender gives us a clear, deep place for our problems to be seen. When we couple surrender with patience, which is a source of comfort, we can live as spiritual beings in the human experience. We are the children of our own choices and lives. If we use spiritual technology, we may eventually realize that innate divinity is our natural state. The ability to tolerate diversity in the world will have more meaning as we become familiar with the art of surrendering. We can learn to surrender, trust what goes on in the mind, and hold only what is accessed from the divine mind. Surrender becomes an important tool once we realize that resisting or fighting to overcome human nature only creates a circuitous route that reinforces its hold. Denying any part of who we are leaves us incomplete. The level of consciousness the natural mind normally exists in is not interested in changing, and it appears to be a space of thought we create to keep us busy in a world perceived as lacking. If everything is part of a divine plan to evolve, all aspects of the personal self can be raw materials for growth. This apparent state of ignorance has led to many practices, rituals, and beliefs in an attempt to hold on to an elusive safety net. In an attempt to avoid sinking into the mire of the natural mind's primitive defensive structures, no matter how anchored we are in ritual, we can inevitably be drawn back into that which creates only conflict and confusion. These learned and limited beliefs and practices serve perfectly in a dualistic learning environment to teach us what works and what doesn't. We continue to put much of our efforts into doing things in the outside world as opposed to focusing on getting to know our natural mind's limitations. Once we become aware of these limits, we can surrender them for a new mindset that feels new and can access more joy. Surrender is a tool of undoing and only requires the letting go of what we once thought we couldn't live without. When one surrenders, one becomes willing to allow others or other beliefs to be in control.

We can let go of outdated thoughts, practices, and behaviors in stages or at once. This multifaceted tool is so versatile that it can be used in any and all challenges. The endeavor of using perception, with its past programming and its limitations, can actually increase the development of a steadfast willingness and devotion to spiritually evolve. However, ultimately, it will always lead to the same frustrating impasse due to its inability to move us forward. No matter the fuel for the striving for fulfillment, whether it be fear, lack, or love, we might still need anchors and weapons to return to for safety. This regression might be beneficial if it reinforces how fruitless old skills can be.

Once we become familiar with surrendering and incorporate it into our toolboxes for spiritual evolution, we will find a warm embrace. Spiritual seekers are often faced with emotional triggers and spiritual challenges that leave them feeling vulnerable and clinging to what might feel like outdated and limited human tools. Rituals, petitions, prayers, manipulation, aggressiveness, and thoughts of victimhood or attack reinforce a self in which there is no escape. To surrender these relics is to trust and allow faith to be the guide. Previously, we trusted in things others taught, and they were reinforced through constant usage. These outdated rituals and thought structures gave us technology that served as stepping-stones that can be seen and measured. This past learning will take us out of alignment with the Self and obscure any appreciation and awareness of our own divine heritage and spiritual worthiness. This becomes evident when we look at the types of relationships created when we believe we can be punished or separated from our own source. The natural mind would perceive our being like a sunbeam separated from the sun: it would just fail to be. One of the immediate benefits of using surrender is that we are less compelled by fear-based motivation and more drawn to change once love moves into place. If we can see that there are only two emotional states and that fear is the absence of love, once fear is surrendered, there is only love.

It is imperative to constantly remind ourselves that the Self is the divine in us and the essence of soul. Soul is not at the mercy of anything in the world of form and change. This is reinforced because of surrender's inherent ability to invoke feelings of resolution and peace, which are fleeting in the world but lie deep in the eternal stillness of our being. It takes great diligence and courage to surrender daily issues, whether they are extreme or mundane. Once we feel this love and have more certainty in our divine heritage, we begin to rely less on fear-based tools. We feel less separation from the divine source. Surrendering also teaches us new levels of trust as we feel more certainty in being guided. Surrender is the energy that drives faith, because it requires focusing on whom and what we trust, and it requires letting go of outcomes. This leap of faith through the door of trust takes a courageous heart filled with a vibration of orange (self-strength) and red (power). Visualizing colors while meditating can also help with the centering process. Once we begin to allow ourselves to surrender, things we might have been using as resistances to hearing divine guidance can drop away. Journeying with divine intention without regard for outcome and direction will increase awareness of Self-certainty.

It is difficult but imperative to realize that even self-destructive behavior can be divinely inspired. Some of these apparent blocks take the form of resentments, low self-esteem, and the belief in lack or victimhood of any kind. We might begin to acquire sacred hope and promise within the unfamiliar and initially vulnerable terrain of misdirection. Once we develop a familiar relationship with our divine consciousness, we can see the beauty of what comes out of the heart of grace. One of these gifts is a divine promise held in the eternal vortex of Self. This promise is analogous to a bank account that already has all the money promised, cashed, and available for usage.

Surrender especially comes in handy during introspection as we bravely accept and dislodge the darkness. Once we surrender with humility and stay anchored in the neutral witness state of mind, our inefficient beliefs, programmed resentments, and self-attack experiences come to the surface and heal. To help with this vital evolutionary practice, imagine surrendering and standing naked—disrobed of your costumes, excuses, and defenses. It is natural for the mind to perceive nakedness as vulnerability, but once we begin to experience Self and feel its certainty, this occurrence becomes easier. Being that vulnerable would be intolerable and rarely attempted if we were not standing in the brilliance of the light or clothed in Self. This light comes from an unrelenting belief in our divinity and the unconditional support available through love. The sacred love that calls us forth in the willingness to believe in our innate holiness gives us the courage to surrender all that tempts us into giving up on our goals. Sometimes we have to fake it to make it. We can even dare to believe that enlightenment, in all its variations, is our inheritance as children of the divine.

The revelation that is apparent once we surrender the journey itself is the realization that our awakening is always by the grace of the divine and is not something earned. The deeper and more frequently we surrender along the journey to peace and the more we use this tool to create this place of mental stillness, the better it works. It is like living at the edge of a cliff of unknowing and jumping off without concern for the landing. We feel deep security in the certainty and inevitability that the landing will be perfect. We might not always get what we want or feel it in expected ways, but we will always get what we need in order to flourish.

The natural mind, with its fear-based survival skills, wants to constantly control the whole journey. Our use of any spiritual tool succeeds through our efforts to bypass these thoughts and our continued vigilance. As we grow accustomed to using spiritual tools, it is normal—and appropriate—to rely on old tools. It is helpful to be patient with the integration of truth and the technologies for living spiritually on earth. If we need to regress, we must leave a trail of bread crumbs. Regression is a teaching tool, as it utilizes contrast perfectly, and should not be used as an excuse to beat oneself up. We have poor understanding at times about what's best for the completion of our soul mission. Something that looks like a regression might be the result of a major step forward and needed for safety in the newness occurring. This supposed step backward or mistake could be just the thing that gives clarity to a wiser choice in the future. The evolutionary journey is always showing us where to go and where love exists in its dualistic fashion, but often, it is obscured.

Certain attitudes, practices, and experiences can increase our confidence and courage as we progress. Dedication, devotion, faith, prayer, surrender, and inspiration can move us past any barriers to an existing knowledge base where truth awaits. Living consciously as we utilize open listening and spiritual vision will help us see the divine in all that the eternal brings. Awakening is the process through which a shift from perception to spiritual vision occurs. New paths open for us. While nothing external has changed, everything is different. Imagine surrendering your control and expectations of all experiences and relationships in your life. When we learn to travel with trust and use surrender as a way to be guided by a divine mind that can see the whole picture, we develop confidence in being spiritually inspired. We will then be more able to see divine signs in all things, even tragedies and challenges we previously judged to be dark. Surrendering can mean allowing occasional periods of regression into old behavior that must now be undone. Attacks, self-will, and faithlessness can also be lessons. Regression brings increasing suffering, and this conflict becomes more tedious.

We can then put more effort into willingness to use higher technology, and less undoing is needed.

As we become more aware of being spiritually guided, we gain more confidence in the process of evolution. It becomes even more appealing if we can see the journey as one that has guaranteed a good ending. We are already holy on another level. When we glimpse the presence of sacred love, we realize it is not a version of conditional love we see in most relationships. The combination of desperation and this glimpse of consistency in grace helps us move into the unfamiliar with growing trust and an increase in faith. Faithlessness will always limit and attack. Faith removes all limitations and makes us whole. Faithlessness will destroy and separate; faith will unite and heal. As we move forward, we move into the unfamiliar with an uncanny feeling of certainty. Surrender to life! Ready? Try this meditation as an exercise for your thoughts:

> Intend to let go of all you know—all the knowledge, all the structure, and all the earthly belief systems that define your present earth-plane reality.
>
> Feel what you know dropping away from you. Surrender to the unknown. Free-fall into what is.
>
> You cannot find what you do not know in what you do know.
>
> Surrender to what you do not know.
>
> Surrender with the intent of letting the divine guide you. Surrender, and receive what is from a place of open listening.

When we talk about surrender, we must also bring in the device of faith. This brave helper is the prerequisite for any spiritual and psychological searching. Faith is the belief in a more established power, which can be either a visible or invisible entity or experience or something that has yet to emerge as distinguishable. When we use faith, we are using our imaginations to set out a blueprint of what we hope for in our lives. This blueprint allows us to courageously keep stretching our limitations and reaching out hopefully in thoughts, behavior, and situations that will manifest our dreams. In using faith as the condition and impetus to surrender, we are allowing our day to unfold in grace and not at the will of our personal self, with its limited perceptive skills. The natural mind holds the belief it is the author of who we are and what we do. Its flaw, however, is that it is always making choices based on its past memory, limited perceptions, and accumulated knowledge. The past is always using limited previous self-concepts, which can appear at times to act like a critical family member who is invested in keeping us in a past that was limited and cemented in a skewed memory stream. The natural mind also can project the worst-case scenario into any thought of the future and thus cripple us with anxiety. To surrender means to relinquish control of something and to allow the grace inherent in all things to teach us and love us as we journey.

Natural mind builds stress and compulsive thoughts and attitudes in an attempt to run our lives in ways that we hope will give us pleasure and success. This pressure-building mechanism is especially powerful in the lives of addicted people. The natural mind stuffs feelings and builds resentments because it sees life through an often unrealistic lens. When reality doesn't match the preexisting and often unconscious set of expectations, our victim response is activated, and bad behavior or self-destruction is then justified.

To have faith after we surrender means that we allow the unfolding of a relationship, situation, or problem to teach us the lesson we often miss that was always needed. This tool is especially energized by the practice of the mantra "What's the lesson?" or "What's the hidden teaching?" I often ask this in faith through prayer or meditation and await the answer to unfold in the occasion or interaction. I often have to accept how others act and surrender in faith, trying to hold back premature judgment. I also await the lessons inherent in some relationships, as I realize people can be either dark teachers or light teachers. Dark teachers incur painful lessons, and light teachers are reflections of grace. Both divine styles are powerful and helpful once we have spiritual vision in place by which to see. Faith is a knowing way of believing that surrender will ultimately give us the needed outcome and allow for more clarity so we can make better choices with our lives. The use of surrender and its escorts, faith and patience, can bring about the best outcome possible. We can also use surrender as a way of releasing resentments. It allows us to jettison our anger and let forgiveness flow into the situation.

The following breathing exercise, called four-seven-eight, also can release mind and body from the buildup of stress that causes impulsive actions and their consequences: draw breath deep into your lungs for a count of four, hold for a count of seven, and exhale slowly for a count of eight. This exercise lessens tension by physically surrendering air to intentionally let go of the emotions that need to be released.

I still have thoughts that are not efficient, behaviors that are outdated or destructive, and rituals once needed to quell old fears and broken expectations of people and circumstances. My natural mind created these fear-filled templates in an attempt to control what was once a vision of a fear-filled world. We can even write down an unmet expectation and then burn the paper in a safe container to watch the smoke, and troubles, rise into the sky. Surrender, along with faith, can truly allow our higher power to take over as we detach ourselves from things or others that no longer serve us. We can then move into position to be divinely inspired through grace. In surrendering, we allow peace and clarity to help us make better choices and create our lives with love. We can cocreate through surrender to a higher, more knowing force, whether that force is a sponsor, a counselor, or a tried-and-true religious or spiritual technology. We can journey with faith in its more knowing power and eventually be more capable in meeting our needs and becoming the people we want.

> Die while you live! Be utterly dead! Then do as you please! All is good!
> —Shido Munan

CHAPTER 6
HIDDEN TEACHINGS

Problems are opportunities in work clothes.
—**Henry J. Kaiser**

We repeat mistakes to further define the illusion of earthly perfection, and if we can eventually accept and realize mistakes will be strewn throughout our daily lives, we will inevitably not get mired in a version of self-reproach that hinders our learning. We often will repeat, in one form or another, mistakes or behaviors that miss a preexisting expectation, until they have taught us their lesson. As a spiritual seeker intent on evolving my consciousness, I was always looking for direction from the Self. It soon became clear that my highest thought was not *out there*. It was being superimposed on certain experiences, people, and objects by the divine mind of Self, which was bringing it into consciousness to teach me. It was then my job to learn and integrate the lessons. When my spiritual vision became more powerful and clear, I saw direction and guidance in both the mundane and the extreme.

In time, through continued reading and experience, I understood that my lessons were always coming forth for resolution. Though I had little conscious awareness of it, spiritual curriculum affected my daily occurrences and relationships. At any time, I could be evolving on a soul level. Love was in all choices and all around me as I journeyed. It became more understandable to look at life on earth as a school and have gratitude for the things and people I encountered and the experiences I went through. Without external objects or circumstances held in contrast, the personal self could not be reflected back onto my spiritual mirror for more clarity.

Without an external backdrop, we might not become aware of the personality at all. Without others, we would not be likely to dredge up unconscious shadow emotions that then find resolution in forgiveness and healing. The Self always had a chance of being discovered amid my guilt and shame as it became triggered by my actions and relationships that were now in the light of spiritual vision. Thoughts are stored in the natural mind and are rich with experiences. These shadow, or yet undiscovered, aspects are still charged with grace and are waiting to be integrated into their roles as change agents as we evolve. This integration and its revelatory energy help build us into personal vessels of divinity on earth. They bring us to the fulfillment and peace we long for, and they call to us always. This happens only once we put aside victimhood long enough to take responsibility for mistakes that are designed to guide us in the right direction.

For me, an important understanding that arose was that I had to accept I was not a victim in life. My life was a unique participation in a holy curriculum. I was personally responsible for my choice to incarnate into this school of contrast and resistance. When I decided to stop resisting the spiritual perspective, I was shown my lessons in even the most hidden occurrences. This endeavor was wrought with resistance by the natural mind, so I had to keep in mind that life was a gift and not a battle. My natural mind or intellect, in its evolutionary patterning of self-focus for survival and fear-based references, often saw through the lens of being attacked. The victimhood default must be seen as an obstacle by spiritual seekers and passed by, observed, or ignored. This obstacle is the huge block of wood in the proverbial eye. It prevents us from seeing how our blessed lessons unfold in the eternal now of every day. The tendency we have to judge creates a dualistic propensity to see beauty as more desirable than ugliness. We constantly discern and feel the vast discrepancy between joy and pain, the fulfilling and the unfulfilling and meaningless. The pursuit of the one end of the spectrum is mostly a solid pursuit. As we get tired of the inability to escape from this circuitous endeavor, we recognize the truth that our focus must change if we are to increase our spiritual nature and reap the rewards therein.

We are first and foremost spiritual beings living human experiences to learn and evolve. The pursuit of what is not comfortable is imperative. In what we resist and judge as bad, there are teachers cloaked in darkness who smile to us and call for our attention. A great teacher once described it as a bell ringing for prayer. The valuable lessons are mostly hidden so as to protect the fragile, ever-shifting self of the personality. These lessons call like sirens to sailors on the sea, and we sometimes fear them because their calls sound and feel like temptation. Giving in to temptation can get us rejected, abandoned, or wounded, which is the natural mind's nightmare. The brave endeavor to leave our comfort zones to search for peace in any form is a sacred path. Most spiritually growing people explore what benevolently calls to them, which is a good start. But if we are to balance and heal, we must also explore what tempts us. All occurrences are informative. All people are teachers of some sort. Given that our normal vision of life is often through our own repressed material, we must always strive to be aware of the often-projected aspect of the personality to move forward toward peace. That which calls us gently beckons us on the heart and soul level to follow. That which tempts us strokes our egos and moves our personality to follow. Notice how quickly and blindly we run toward what calls us. Why do we trust this urge? Notice how quickly and strongly we resist what tempts us. Why do we not trust this urge? In the stillness and fertility of neutral witness, we can clearly see aspects of the personal self that need to be healed, balanced, and forgiven. If we know what tempts us as clearly as we know what calls us, we increase compassion and then become unconditional conduits on earth. There is a secret to integrating this knowledge for ourselves and for others. That which calls us is the same as that which tempts us. It is clothed in a different guise. To know what tempts us in the calling and what calls in the temptation is the goal. Here's a hint: it is all the same—the struggle to evolve.

This important chapter resumes our discussion on the limitations of human perception. If we do not understand that our visions come through the eyes of our past issues and experiences, we presume that our natural mind is telling us all that is true. In doing so, we always come back to ourselves when we journey for revelation. This is limiting. Spiritual people are always being challenged to trust in the divinity inherent in the journey, not in what they think they know. We presume our intellectual knowledge is relevant to our growing awareness and evolution as individuals. Letting go of complete reliance on the knowledge we have acquired is a leap of faith. To stop running for more knowledge is to surrender to the ever-present teacher in all.

I personally had to acquire more knowledge for curiosity's sake, not revelation, which meant I had to trust in the divine timing of my lessons. I came to realize that major steps in my conscious growth just happened. My revelations became much clearer, and so did my understanding of the process of becoming awakened. It came from outside my line of vision and the things I had seen and known. This taught me more faith and trust. I began to understand that revelation and evolution happened when information from outside my previous knowledge collided with my life experience. People, experiences, and knowledge in the form of books, quotes, and media events also spontaneously appeared. I realized that my options for evolution emerged from an infinite source that was both within and without. This truly enlightened curriculum was attracted from a desire to evolve and move into a Self where peace reigned supreme. The obstacles inherent in perception must be constantly observed through neutrality. When we go within, we find variations of the natural mind's programming blocking our perceptions. Presence, in its undiscovered brilliance, is at hand deep within, but it is the part of us that is plugged into the infinite potential in Self only.

To help with my human eyes' penchant for obscuring the divine knowledge being communicated constantly, I began to journal. I wrote down the dark, resisted thoughts. Their expression allowed for a level of awareness that opened my ability to hear the divine more clearly and build an attitude of unconditional acceptance toward the personal self and life. Another way of staying vigilant to the revelations moving us forward is to read our own journals and frequently revise our spiritual goals. Then we can recommit through the laws of attraction to manifest our desires. Spirituality can also mean fulfillment in our lives through material security and relationship love. One should perform this journaling habit mostly upon wakening and at bedtime. Phrases and repetitive thought streams help solidify the manifestations as they grow the depth of belief needed for earth appearances. I found these to also be a major tool in calling forth the Self as we grow in dedication to our ultimate purpose, which is to transcend any and all obstacles to living in peace, love, and joy.

Full acceptance and the acceptance of the dark sides of my natural mind and personal self became valuable agents in my life and cornerstones of growth. I discussed my feelings of hatred, apathy, revenge, sadness, guilt, shame, fear, and loneliness. I called this dredging of my conscious, preconscious, and unconscious *the wasteland*. My teacher explained how this helps to express the inherent guilt we all live with. I realized I was repeating patterns and creating repercussions that sapped my joy and peace and possibly created physical illness. By expressing my hatred in either meditation or journaling and by allowing dark thoughts to be expressed verbally in prayer or in person, I could see their fruitlessness through neutrality. I eventually realized that writing not only served as an avenue to vent but also activated centers in my brain that wouldn't normally have been helpful in creating a creative healing process fueled by unconscious sources. By journaling and externalizing hidden feelings, I could see how real-life drama distracted my growth and led to a delay in evolution. By seeing it in writing without judgment or shame, I could intend to move away from any observed harmful patterns. In writing down goals, strengths, weaknesses, and positive movements forward, I increased my willingness to accept any hidden shame and stored guilt sapping my joy. When I tried to repress the revenge-attack patterns by hiding the thoughts, I was only hiding from my alleged enemies. I still harbored hatred and, ultimately, projected vengeance toward them or others who reminded me of them. The battle was still on, and I began to feel out of sync and tethered.

The wasteland is one tool of externalization that has many ways of allowing us to move past our own resistance to accept our resistance to peace. In a dualistic world, it is helpful to remember that once aware of our darkness, we are more likely to move and act from our light. Hidden teachings are afoot in everything. We have a choice to either develop the eyes to see or remain in obscurity from the divine teachings gifted through grace. Even though I rarely acted on the dark propensities, my natural mind carried them as ribbons of personal self. They must be brought to the table and loved for balance. They cannot be sidestepped or denied. These defensive tactics delay our joy and the development of a more efficacious personality.

Once we give ourselves the option to see the focus of attention on the happenstances of our lives as a perfect, timely way of learning, then spiritual vision can act as a great helper. When we look at our earthly equipment, we see that we really have donned four bodies: physical, mental, emotional, and spiritual. We cannot afford to neglect looking at any of them for lessons that contain either joy or misalignment. When we are feeling emotionally fulfilled, physically vibrant, or mentally clear, the lesson might be to look at the map that got us there. If we are bankrupt spiritually, filled with resentment, and looking for conflict, then the teaching is hidden in projections and attack protocol. Whether through joy, love's fulfillment, love's absence, suffering, or fear, we are being taught to keep our human and spiritual lives on track. We must always remember that the journey of our personal self is as important as our Self. Both lead us to soul evolution, which is the ultimate goal.

Even sickness can bring us into a full view of discordance. Its onset is not used as a whipping stick by either the Self or the misalignments of the natural mind, but we must focus on choices concerning things we carry in our minds that affect us physically or emotionally.

The emotional body has been the most complicated in my journey. I have had a penchant for toxic shame and guilt, which has motivated my actions since I was young. These dark teachers kept me somewhat in line socially, but they created a lack of authenticity and a tendency toward self-flogging seen in the programming of low self-esteem. This led to my having to escape pain before performing any task that was risky. Escape took on many forms, from substance abuse to people-pleasing, and all of them reinforced a world flecked with guilt and shame. This eventually led to periods of procrastination and living the status quo in my life. I eventually learned that healthy shame and appropriate guilt, along with seeing all emotions as teachers and vibrant forms of soul communication, were the hidden gifts in this lesson. As it became clear that my goal as a spiritual seeker was to become a healing force on earth, I realized these emotions had to be understood for their divine underbellies. My healing power evolved through the true resolution of guilt, unworthiness, and the revelations I received spiritually. My deeper understanding of the unity of all things rendered my personal self integral and needed, not primary. In guilt and unworthiness, the personal self is primary, and the maintenance of the status quo is justified. The resolution of unworthiness, shame, and guilt gives life vibrancy each day, as it is a constant source of self-love and compassion. Once I realized that suffering and joy were best brought on by relationships as personal teachers, I decided to evolve with willingness.

There is no way to get this journey wrong. There are no wrong turns with eyes wide open. Every step taken is one step closer to spiritual fulfillment, whether it appears to take the traveler forward or backward. The physical body becomes a perfect reflection of the traveler's path, a perfect map to look for clues to what the traveler must heal. The spiritually minded seeker sees all occurrences in neutrality as light or dark, all feelings as information, and all people as messengers and perfect mirrors. The body is a gift and a source of valuable information. A damaged heart can mean the spiritual journey is taken on the path of the heart, and love is the theme. Circulatory issues hint to seekers to clearly define where they are going on their journeys. High blood pressure calls travelers to look at the actions not taken, and diabetes asks travelers to fully explore their general relationship to sweetness. One can never forget that we will eventually see the divine interior in all things. Through spiritual vision, love is fully and unconditionally ours, even if the natural mind's default is victimhood, shame, or guilt. With open eyes and receptive hearts, the sacred can be seen in all. The sacred is always working to be seen, and even though one of our four bodies might be in a dark lesson, faith in the concept that life is happening for us will help.

> Tragedy is a tool for the living to gain wisdom, not a guide by which to live.
> —Robert F. Kennedy

CHAPTER 7
UNCONDITIONALITY

Unconditional love is a precious goal and a gift while on earth. The earth school, with its laws of cause and effect and duality, sets up many conditions and challenges that serve as a curriculum for learning. These perfect laws reveal the edges to all our choices and constantly point to who and what we are and where we are going on the spiritual journey. In order to progress in this world of conflict, one needs milestones and indicators to offer direction and feedback. If perception, by nature, is faulty because of its too-personal biases, in order to learn our divinely inspired and supported lessons, we need all types of reflective devices to assess how we are doing and what is in front of us. One of the most precious of the spiritual technologies presented in this book is the healing vessel of unconditionality.

This sacred mindset is an expression that includes unconditional love, but it is more of a soul expression than dualistic counterpart. If there is unconditional love, there must be conditional love as well. This makes unconditionality more of a natural-mind tool than a being state. This perfect higher-mind energy system acts much like joy and divine love. They have no dualistic counterparts.

For many of us, the initial practice of unconditionality is intense and complicated due to our misunderstanding of the difference between being and doing. I read about spiritually enlightened beings and advanced teachers being unconditionally loving. That practice did not work often for a person from a struggling family who grew up programmed in a completely conditional environment. I was measured by extreme conditions and rewarded when they were met. Many times, I held on too long in painfully conditional relationships. I was constantly afraid I would fall short and be rejected. I felt the hell of conditionality while reading about unconditional love and listening to sermons that proclaimed its necessity. If I was to become Self, I had to learn that unconditionality was an intentioned mind state that held all journeys as sacred all the way to their core, even while recognizing that other journeys might not be about love at all. I eventually realized that an unexamined life was a constant assessment of conditions and judgments made in the hope of navigating each hurdle adequately. If we are to share hearts of unconditionality, we must accept all that happens as divinely inspired. This powerful tool is a state of heart that shows love for all expressions of belief without judgment. In this case, whenever we refer to heart, we are looking at an aspect of divine mind that holds all the most beloved things in perfect innocence.

The pain of not reaching the bar of safety in each relationship and the many rules of success I was taught about life were my battlefield of pleasure and pain. I saw a world that reflected my growing belief in conditional existence as a rule. I saw competition as the status quo, and rejection and humiliation were the hangmen when I lost. I had such shame and guilt that my mind was a prison house of judgment in which I tried to find relief in a world of changing expectations and apparent deceit. These early experiences were the proving ground for my learning spiritually based technologies. My previous broken programming, which created my extreme longing for peace and my devotion to spirituality, was my family experience as a child. My parents' relationship was my first battleground, and my mother's drinking made the pain worse. This early experience made my codependency acute and triggered negative emotions often. After much healing, I have much gratitude for the compassion that was born. Eventually, with much contemplation and healing, I was given a great revelation about the nature of dualistic learning. It moved me further on the path of peace and unconditionality. I realized I could not have known what I knew without experiencing its opposite. The ability to learn important concepts, such as harmony, true neutrality, unconditional love, and nonduality, was the gift of living with contrast and becoming awake to duality as a predominant law of spiritual evolution.

As I began to heal, first and foremost, I had to learn more about self-forgiveness and self-kindness. I struggled in painful self-judgments as I tried to fit the pursuit of unconditionality into a conflicted multilayered mind that included an intellectual belief in both unconditional love and self-attack. The natural mind clings to its precious, fragile self-image with stubbornness. These uses for judgment were based on conscious and unconscious conditions I had yet to fully grasp. Because they remained unconscious, they played out in my daily life. I was constantly giving to get and seeking revenge when slighted. I hated people, animals, past events, objects, and future experiences in the now because they did not meet up with unrecognized expectations. My mind raced to judgment and took pleasure when revenge was observed or meted out. Revenge usually came in the form of angry thoughts or blame.

I was not successful in completely shaking conditional thinking, but I soon had two helpful revelations: (1) personally, we cannot require others to be loving, kind, grateful, or spiritual for us to respect them and call them friends, and (2) socially and professionally, we cannot require kindness or civility to assist someone in healing. Once using true neutrality became more automatic, I could apply it to the voice of conditional responses. I watched as many things throughout my day fell short or went against my conditions. I was not even aware of some of the conditions, but they were exposed in my reactions to particular people or situations. In the neutral witness, I could observe how my natural mind needed to constantly define its edges and solidify its specialness and separateness through these conditions, which required constant upkeep. I extended love easily, but I expected love in many forms in return. True neutrality showed me the insanity inherent in that practice and how often it robbed me of peace.

To make this advanced mindset of unconditionality more prevalent, we can shift our beliefs in love to align with what we are feeling in the eternal now, adjust our conditional dualistic tendencies, and use the following advanced guidelines in the light of neutral eyes:

1. The intolerable does not exist.
2. Everything is exactly as it is intended to be.
3. Everyone is absolutely perfect in his or her life's journey.
4. Nobody is going anywhere; he or she has already arrived.
5. The demand for gratitude negates the original gesture.

6. You are what you see and what you do not.
7. You are what you reject and what you do not.
8. You are what you believe and what you do not.
9. To fear is to resist the divine flow of what is.
10. To be fearless is to resist the divine flow of what is.

In changing through the constant use of these thought redirections, I began to entertain the thought that love was a personal inheritance and not a bartering tool. I realized I was given consciousness as love, and the clearer the divine mind's voice became with its whisper of inner love, the better my joy and peaceful experiences would become. I learned to extend love without allowing the natural mind's fear-filled voice for conditions to dictate choices. I could observe my conditionality and choose unconditionality as an option.

My past relationships had a lot to do with how I reacted to everyone in the present. Projection is always relevant in relationships. We have relationships with all things in life, but people are the most complicated. Our interactions with careers and objects can be intricate, but our relationships with people continue to penetrate our hearts. That's why our perception or understanding of why people do what they do is of supreme interest. Sacred others are powerful teachers because of the roles they play and the messages they bring. An angel once visited me in a dream and said, "All journeys are divine. If you cannot find love for all others, then you are not seeing their truth." If a sacred other shows up in my life as any form of teacher, either light or dark, bringing either pleasure or pain, I attempt to see his or her presence as an inspiration and a potentially fertile opportunity for balance and healing.

The earth is a place to heal the inherent feeling of separation and all the unconscious fear and guilt programmed into the natural mind. I have learned that our interactions with others are efficient at highlighting our fear-based characteristics as well as the divine abilities and gifts hidden deep within us. At one time, my shame and guilt were so deep that without an external trigger, I was unwilling and unlikely to bring out my repressed fear, anger, and ignorance, which blocked gifted skills from being accepted and transformative. When we are vigilant in relationships, others become teachers set up to help us see ourselves as we evolve. This practice of a higher spiritual awareness makes room for the Self by direct intention and welcomes the courageous heart to stay devoted to spiritual technology. The Self has clarity that the natural mind, with its finite memory, does not have.

As with all learning on earth, how you receive and integrate what is being taught daily determines how your life unfolds. There is no wrong way to interpret your life's happenstances, but some ways are more enriching. It is imperative that we use some particular spiritual technology (e.g., neutral witness, surrender, and humility) as a constant centering practice to deliver us from a limiting and confusing perception. We must fully understand that all vision becomes clearer through the introspective eyes of our life experiences. If we assume that our natural eyes tell us all that is, we will always come back to ourselves as reference, no matter where we journey for revelation. This is limiting, especially in relationships. In relationships, we are constantly challenged to trust what we do not know and presume it is relevant to who we are and what we are becoming.

Many people are not versed in terms like *transference*, *perception*, and *projection* and don't realize that the natural mind is limited by several factors and relies on previous programming. It searches desperately for answers in pursuit of peace, resolution, or control, which might never be found, fulfilled, or sustained.

Once we realize that normal thinking and vision are limited, we are closer to being able to discern truth from falsehood. When we use surrender and neutrality to journey with faith in the care of our divine mind as a guide, we begin to trust that the journey is on track, whether we feel suffering or joy. We can then navigate relationships with two missions in mind: (1) meeting natural needs and (2) satisfying spiritual longings. Since a good part of this journey relies on relationships to meet these needs, we have to integrate both the natural world and the spiritual world with compassion.

The spiritual seeker of today is usually a busy householder who has chosen to be in the middle of modern life. We have to find time for spiritual study and practice while meeting the needs of social existence. This dualistic cauldron is perfect for extreme levels of evolution because the amount of interaction is increased, and we are constantly forced out of our comfort zones. There is no escape from our projections because they come from inside our minds and are looking for objects on which to shine. The intention to see how we are being mirrored in our relationships helps us in several important ways. Whether we accept it or not, we are constantly getting feedback about who we are and how we can become more socially pliable. As we walk through our day, we are given constant opportunities to trigger hidden, repressed obstacles to our spiritual goals. We are constantly drawn to people who make us feel good or trigger repressed, previously judged aspects of our personal self we fear or hate. We assume they are both safe havens.

I eventually excelled at creating some safe relationships, but I was constantly being challenged to be in relationships that were not comfortable. I realized that thinking of them with respect made these dark teachers a must if I was to reach my goal of becoming a fully functional vessel of divine love. I use the word *dark* in this context not as an evil description but as a moniker for a relationship that teaches mostly through discomfort and suffering. Learning in these relationships became a priority, and navigating them daily was next on the curriculum to learn. I had previously used unfulfilling tools, such as dishonesty, attack, manipulation, escapism, and blame, to hide my need for control. Judgments and resentments stole my peace. My next lesson was integrating the truth that I actually attracted these beings as curriculum in a school I had designed through previous choices for my optimal learning. This also meant I was never a victim. I practiced coming from the storehouse of my Self-love to the point where I could stay in pain-filled relationships longer to learn their meaning. You can do this only when the source of love you draw from is more internal than external. I did not physically have to hold on to the toxic social interaction any longer in order to resolve unfinished feelings or manipulate external situations, but still, I started experiencing either revelations or gratitude for the other being, no matter the end circumstances.

Throughout much of my childhood, adolescence, and young adulthood, suffering was the result of one mental and karmic construct: "If the world loves me, I know I am loved." The need for outside love and safety leaves many of us frustrated and angry. I tried to procure love from others who were not always ready or interested in love as an agenda. This trial led to the following revelations:

1. Release your enemies to live their own lives. Let go of previous relationship battle plans. Allow others to not like you.
2. Allow yourself to not be friends with everyone.

3. You are obligated to love your enemies enough to respect their unique expressions of life.
4. Extend all the love you want to anyone, but expect nothing in return. (You expect a return because you are trying to reinforce your own safety and value.)

Not all sacred missions are about love. I saw that I spent much of my social energy hiding from the world in shame or manipulating those I loved. When I felt safe or self-loving, the feeling was anchored not in me but in how the outside world received me. I was also at the mercy of perceiving others' reactions to me or my behavior through a lens of guilt and shame. These painful chronic states of mind were remnants of my ingrained belief that I had somehow been a cause or a toxic part of the trauma of my childhood. This perception created a closed loop of suffering. However, to balance these chronic thought streams, I was given many light teachers in my life. They were prevalent and took many forms. They came from coaching relationships, family, and friends.

These eventually expanded to other sacred teachers, including schoolteachers, professors, colleagues, clients, movies, books, and experiences. Romantic relationships also brought lessons of light and dark and played a significant role in teaching. The lure of physical attraction and feelings of sexuality facilitated the safety and security of having one special companion.

As I became more aware of the dark and light aspects inherent in self through journaling, discussions with my teachers, and prayer, I learned that I am like everyone else. Sacred teachers give us many lessons; it seemed that all my hidden darkness began to emerge to be forgiven, mostly in relationships. The sacred others closest to me were the greatest mirrors, and even if my interactions with them were in the past, I could bravely follow the bread crumbs back to what seemed like a tortuous uncovering. This happened as I contemplated and journaled about my journey. Forgiving the past was healing me in the present, and as I became more aware of the projections I saw through and the attractions I kept calling forth, I was constantly forced to forgive, surrender, and change my mind to believe the pain was perfect for my growth. This allowed me to be more authentic in my new and present relationships and to make better choices. People I came to know and let pass through my life were like seasons. A season is an experience and a time frame that has boundaries and limits. Each season served as fertile ground for my growth for a period, and it was then pushed out by the next one. There were no incomplete journeys; I viewed them all as sacred and helpful. No matter how they were presented or the nature of the interactions, I could retreat to true neutrality and witness the divinity present in each and every sacred other.

One of the biggest obstacles to my seeing others through a spiritual vision that allowed for kindness and growth was the lens of injustice. The natural mind constantly works from a default of filling and emptying with others or objects. I mistakenly believed they were the primary source of my lack or my fulfillment. This tendency was a stubborn leftover from a personal self that had to constantly define itself at the expense of others and things: "I'm not that," "I have this, and you don't," "I am more," or "I am less." The need to use comparison, recognition, remembrance, and reward requires constant vigilance if we are to gain ground spiritually. I brought this self-darkness to my teacher, and the following truth changed my view of the blockage: *I am where I am for fighting to be right. I cannot bear to be treated unjustly.* I apparently was missing the point. *Injustice is based on the belief that I hold the truth.*

I realized the trick was that something is either a spiritual truth or a falsity. Anything that defined my personal self was false, transparent, or a piece of something. The premise was and is that there are no half-truths. The human self is a cover or a vessel that must be transcended and set aside. That's why there is no way to perfect it. There is no way out! This brings on the Self. That is where the spirit can guide us. There is no injustice to resolve. We cannot be treated unjustly or even justly if everything is perfect the way it is. Everything serves the highest good. Can we celebrate being treated justly? Watch your answer.

Once we see others from a higher perspective, it becomes easier to navigate and negotiate what seems like two worlds. Through spiritual vision, we can choose to drop our neediness in relationships. We learn Self-reliance. We do not idolize and give our power away to human demigods, but we still see their sacred relevance and retain respect for their missions. Even though all are unique, we are all one and can love or choose to fearfully project our issues onto others. Others might act in certain ways that disturb us, but this is meant to teach us and trigger the wisdom below the surface of perception. If you are in a relationship, remember that resonance joins like mind and like soul together. If you assume mediocrity, you will receive dullness. Nothing is done for such people to know each other. If you have issues to be resolved or learn, you are sending out signals right now to a teacher. Light or dark, all teachers are of divine inspiration. They have the potential to move you beyond and above the battlefield. Look at the people you are drawing into your life, and ask what they are teaching you about yourself. Once you see it, forgive yourself, and change it if that is your will. We create our relationships on levels we cannot imagine. All are perfect for the greater good. Everyone is acting in this scene of your life. See the divine light in their eyes. See it in their actions, and hear it when they speak. Everyone is playing the divine for you. Watch them, and learn the knowingness of spirit and Self.

To truly enhance our use and understanding of unconditionality, we must become more acquainted with the energy of unconditional love. To begin to use unconditional love as a proper escort to the mindset of unconditionality, we must first see the nature of love with different eyes. Our usual concept of love consists of a conditional bartering system with all aspects of our experience. We receive and give love to ourselves, others, pets, jobs, nature, and God. We function under the tenuous understanding that feeling loved is leased inside and outside to external powers that often are not interested or aware of our needs. Some believe these powers may even be invested in creating suffering for us through their hidden agenda.

I used to feel loved in church or after playing well in sports or getting praised at work. This system of conditional love always left me with an uneasy feeling. The spiritual helper of unconditional love begins and ends with our acceptance of the concepts that we are love and that love is not a commodity that can be lessened in any way. Love is like our biological heritage. I am Irish, and no matter how I feel, think, or act, my Irish heritage cannot be lessened or increased in any way. To maintain self-love in the unconditional mindset, I need only to have a decent regret, own the challenge, and take responsibility for any action or shortcoming. By finding a more effective behavior, I not only undo the consequence but also gain wisdom.

The love that exists in the unconditionality mindset begins to enhance our concept of self-love immediately. We can now love all aspects of our personalities, essential traits, personal stories, and physical conditions. The learning really begins when we come face-to-face with our experiences and personality traits that are mean, cruel, or weak with fear. To love ourselves unconditionally, we must embrace ourselves in the context that we are of loving origin and holy lineage. I began to see that my mistakes and character flaws were there because I believed I needed them in order to meet my needs at that time. I began to accept negative qualities, such as my insecurity and anger, because they were important tools in my transformation to be secure and peaceful. The qualities that previously had brought me pain through shame and guilt eventually became doorways to new qualities and even doorways to compassion for others. By my adjusting existing fear-based, negative behavior, my qualities are often transformed into the opposite of what they once were. For example, I used to be impatient with my children's loud play, until I created a personal signal to calm down. I would become more patient and nurturing by putting my hands on my heart and extending a vibration of tolerance as they played or tested my mood.

After watching an episode of *Seinfeld*, I created the teaching term *opposite day* to explain the daily activity of turning vice into virtue. I first recognize through vigilance that I am coming from a dark mood; then I do the opposite. The following centuries-old spiritual technology illustrates the transformational wisdom of using existing egoistic limitations to catapult us to our Self.

Prayer of Saint Francis

Lord, make me an instrument of your peace.
Where there is hatred, let me sow love.

Where there is injury—pardon. Where there is discord—unity. Where there is doubt—faith.

Where there is error—truth. When there is despair—hope.

Where there is sadness—joy. Where there is darkness—light. O divine master,

grant that I may not seek to be consoled as to console, to be understood as to understand,

to be loved as to love, for it is in giving that we receive.

It is in pardoning that we are pardoned.

Through unconditionally loving myself, I was able to honestly examine my use of fear-based choices. This helped to show me the road to change through the uncovering of the repeated futility of my actions. I hated bad drivers, rude people, and dependent clients, but as I became more adept at introspection, I eventually saw these qualities were also present in my personal self, but I judged the qualities into repressed oblivion only to attract them again in others. I eventually saw myself as a perfect mansion under construction and accepted all rooms, gardens, and cesspools as perfect for my life and for the development of compassion. I would externalize my worst qualities, thought processes, and fears in an attempt to uncover them in prayer, on paper, or by telling them to others. I then began to love myself, not in spite of these theoretically unlovable parts but because of them. I now saw them as a way to gain true internal peace and to see my neighbor as my Self, thus communing with them in a deeper, more satisfying way.

Unconditional love allowed me to have more compassion for mistakes made by my children and my wife. This gave me more patience to make better and more loving choices to help others or just hold the space in loving regard. Love became something I brought with me everywhere, and when I let it be covered by fear, I felt coldness. I then had to go back inside to look for and at the existing unloved and unworthy remnants of my beliefs about myself. I constantly worked at removing all resentments and revisited the lessons learned from the past instead of remaining a victim whose love energy was drained by residual anger and fear. Holding the spiritual mindset of unconditionality allows complete freedom from lingering states of shame or guilt. The emotional body is then freed up to be only a teacher, not a punisher.

I once did an exercise in which I identified the qualities about myself I felt were negative and looked at them as if they were children trapped in dark rooms in my house. Through a meditative guided tour, I went to each room and brought all the children to the table for a meal of forgiveness. This guided healing works tremendously to feel the power of atonement.

While reading *A Course in Miracles*, I began to see myself as an aspect of God and began feeling that I was, as the book says, "whole already." That was how I began to think of myself in my heart. The brave use of the escort tool of unconditional love helps us recognize our real state of wholeness and being and brings us closer to living in the mindset of unconditionality. When this is extended to others, it can take many forms but never creates a thought of lack in the natural mind. This intention and its activity in our lives signal the flowering of Self. When we are given love from an outside source, it is a reflection of our heritage of love, as if someone is holding up a clear mirror of us to enjoy. Eventually, all creation becomes a mirror of this unconditional love. Even the darker emotions and occurrences are transformed into teachers and are welcomed, not avoided.

The following poem of love from my favorite ancient mystic further illustrates that spiritual vision is timeless and always relevant. The following centuries-old spiritual technology is also another great depiction of the integration of how unconditional love becomes unconditionality.

The Guest House

This being human is a guest house.
Every morning a new arrival.
A joy, a depression, a meanness,
Some momentary awareness comes
As an unexpected visitor.
Welcome and entertain them all!
Even if they're a crowd of sorrows,
Who violently sweep your house
Empty of its furniture,
Still, treat each guest honorably.
He may be cleaning you out
for some new delight.
The dark thought, the shame, the malice,
Meet at the door laughing,
And invite them in.
Be grateful for whoever comes,
Because each has been sent,
As a guide from beyond.

—Jalal ad-Din Rumi

CHAPTER 8
HANDLING FEARFUL THINKING

For significant spiritual growth, only one simple tool is required. It is merely necessary to select any simple principle that is appealing and then proceed with its application, without exception, to every area of your life, both within and without.
—David R. Hawkins, MD, PhD

An important priority of spiritual searchers in a world of finite form can be what has no end. Once this is seen, we can better discern what we think is important. How can we obtain abstract spiritual goals and measure things in a realm of constant change and blurry perceptions unless we are aware of our thoughts and use contrast as a device to see both how we are doing and what has yet to be aspired to?

In this school of earth, we are constantly challenged to move in faith and search in darkness for long periods. This moves us to discuss a priority of focus that can add major measurable progress to our lives. The monitoring and constant adjustment of fear-minded thinking is one of the spiritual technologies with the most power, considering that these thoughts often have a fear-based origin and naturally create the worst consequences. This power lies in how we observe past perceptions that have created previous suffering. Through vigilance, we stay aware of internal dialogue and feelings that are signals for us to make wise choices. Our thoughts are our best friend or worst obstacle in accomplishing spiritual and personal intentions. What we think and then do to keep and accomplish any Self or personal goal increases confidence during the obscure climb out of darkness to whatever calls us.

To distinguish a Self goal from a personal goal, we must look at its all-inclusiveness and win-win strategy, primarily using our thinking. As you invest in transforming your mind into a more spiritually driven device, you are calling forth a Self that always includes the needs of others and makes choices based on the inherent wisdom only found in love. Understanding the mind of Self and our use of the mind itself becomes the sacred ground by which we traverse the challenges that are soul-designed for evolution. The negotiation of the natural mind in the safety and light of true neutrality gives us the skills to let go of thoughts that can impede our intention to be a healing force for ourselves and others and keeps us in the illusion of separation. In the light of neutrality, we see how certain thoughts are linked to patterns of meaningless and distracting choices that inevitably offer more work for us in their undoing.

I began to see that my most measurable growth happened when I felt more confident in being able to be clear on what was fear-based thinking. I practiced not making choices based on their nonsense. Once I grew clearer on what fear-based thoughts were and what they felt like, the sane and love-minded ones were illuminated. Every time I felt lonely, depressed, or lost, I would use a tool to follow the bread crumbs back to the fearful origin in the thought that held me there. Then, by seeing through contrast, I would search out and experiment with several of the tools mentioned in this book in an attempt to create wise thoughts and their subsequent positive feeling states, which could then carry me out of those painfully limited mind spaces. Love-minded thinking, whether it comes from the best reasoning of the natural mind or is directly inspired from Self, always has a better effect. It creates less work in the world and less suffering in our physical and emotional bodies. We must become skilled bullfighters and avoid the bull of the mind state of fear.

I heard a story about a great hitter with perfect vision. He could see the stitches on the baseball as it left the pitcher's hand. He saw the ball coming the whole way, and he could hit it at will. This is what is created once we get acclimated to seeing our minds as fertile grounds for soul progression and human evolution.

In graduate school and through my subsequent work of integration and transformation through contemplative daily practice and devoted reading, I began to see the obstacles to peace more clearly. The biggest and most relentless was my constant negative self-judgment. I had an analytical mind, but when it was directed at me and my behavior, analysis gave way to judgment. This judgment spawned guilt, and it reinforced any shame that had been formed. The handling of fear-filled thoughts frees the beauty of spiritual vision to observe and sidestep any beliefs that could lead you down a meaningless or destructive path. The Self supports any choice we make, but why go there, when we can focus on the tool of mind management through neutrality? Why not avoid the suffering created by bad choices and dark teachers and take the journey with peace?

As my spiritual life continued to grow, my mind became more adept at allowing my outer life to flow through me for recognition and learning. I learned that my natural mind constantly dealt me a hand made up of thoughts that I often found selfish and mean. As I controlled my mind through various thought and practice exercises, it became easier to sidestep the lure of that which chided me to respond reactively from both outside and inside. I saw occasions to hate, judge, cheat, and lie. Thoughts of resentment, doubt, and fear passed through my mind, as they were now sifted through for their valuable lessons. I addressed and resolved what was stuck, and in most cases, I did not look back at the thought, feeling, or lesson learned. I am constantly working on letting go of the outcome, but I believe earth is a place to develop skills and extend them, not be without occasion to grow. It became more apparent once I absorbed the concept that what is not an extension of loving thought always comes from a place of fear and nothing else. In understanding this blessed tool of mind maintenance, we should be vigilant and informed about the differences between love-mindedness and fear. In dualistic contrast, it became clear that these two completely separate neighborhoods have different missions, and they are motivated by different causes.

Fear-mindedness can be recognized by its previously held beliefs in what is lacking, competitive, and limited. The past rules this house of natural mind; with its conclusions and errors, it navigates the eternal now with a hand that trembles with fear. This thought house is capable of creating the majority of our anger and fear-based emotional experiences. It is a source of poor choices, physical illness, and karmic consequences. This dualistic teacher is actually an absence of the mind of Self. On a good note, its circuitous route of unfulfillment can drive us to be more willing and curious about looking outside our previous program for comfort. The fear-minded perspective is a hodgepodge of diversity and conflict, and it strives to value and judge each thought, decision, and person for its or his or her ability to fulfill a lack. These inherent limitations keep us journeying into a darkness that has only fleeting rewards.

In an earlier chapter, I spoke about the importance of balance in our journeys. This congruence helps create oneness of mind and helps mitigate the conflict in the natural mind, with its penchant for competition and dualistic counterparts. When diversity is recognized, all factors are equally embraced and revered, and there is no lesser or higher choice. In true neutrality, we can have divine clarity. This tool of spiritual vision helps us see through the right mind, allowing us to make wise, reasonable decisions and live as spiritual beings on earth.

When we look at fear-minded thinking, we see specific rules that need to be addressed. For instance, it became clear that I was willing to cling to thoughts as they clung to me. This triggered my victimhood default, which needed to be resolved in some way. I repeatedly let go only to have that default surface in another lesson at another time. This tested my use of surrender and faith as I navigated with trust in divine resolution and the use of wise-minded, inspired wisdom. I realized that wise thinking was being stimulated through the door of balance and neutrality. My Self can see in the darkness a lot better than my natural mind can. This revelation inspired and allowed me to serve from a perspective beyond what appears to be. With wisdom as my guide and with fear thoughts seen and released, creation through love's extension had renewed energy. The extension of love happened in ways beyond my previous hopes. One might even experience illuminated states wherein sufficient barriers have been dropped deliberately or unconsciously. This can bring about a greater context and an inner light that are unforgettable. Spiritual seekers are constantly moving past previous stuck points, even if doing so is not conscious.

This new vessel of happy learning was a host to newness. In this newness, I had the increased energy of patience, faith, and clarity. Out of this fertile ground came the following thought concepts, which, when used daily and remembered in a timely fashion, accentuated the point of mind maintenance. I found the daily use of the following concepts and phrases helpful:

- Let it go.
- Let go to be free.
- Disidentify.
- Disregard.
- Make irrelevant.
- Exchange.
- Make room.
- Tell the self a new story.
- Displace this for that.
- Lay aside.
- Ignore or cancel.
- Dismiss.
- Laugh at.
- Take lightly.
- Be dispassionately involved.

These phrases can be used to allow the flow and ultimate extraction of fear-minded and toxic thoughts, events, and interactions. The logjam that creates pain is loosened, and the stream of higher consciousness flows with force and divine inspiration. Try out each one, and do so without reserve. Laughing at things or taking them lightly is also spiritually inspired and does not have to be used to minimize the responsibility for something. Instead, laughter releases judgment and provides space so divine messages can be seen in their entirety.

In conclusion, it is wonderful to gain any ground in the house of mind. Once we can balance, allow, and tolerate automatically, peace is more available and more present in our lives. This practice gives us balance that allows for glimpses of oneness and the levels of higher consciousness.

> One who conquers himself is greater than another who conquers a thousand times on the battlefield.
> —Buddha

CHAPTER 9
ALL I AM NOT IS ALL I AM BECOMING

You are braver than you believe, stronger than you seem, and smarter than you think.
—A. A. Milne

When we work with this healing paradox, we must first recall the rules of duality. Contrast and measurement help us understand where we were, where we are, and where we will go. Without these backdrops, we have little or no reference in the world of form. We especially have little or no reference to spiritual reality. We might only imagine it in our dreams, connect with it by faith, or hear about it through stories and scripture. To proceed in any meaningful direction, we must leverage a map made up of experiences and associated feelings. This gives us invaluable information for fostering hope and curiosity in the shadows of human life as we grow in confidence, faith, and surrender into our existing potential.

In a therapy session many years ago, a talented young man repeated a line from a poem he had written: "All I am not is all I am becoming." As we spoke, I was impressed that on his own, he had begun to use his anxiety to journal and write poetry to pass the time when panic set in. I brought up the notion that his fear was teaching him faith and that he could lessen physical suffering by reframing the mental experience. We used this concept to conquer many of his misperceptions over the year we worked together. This brave work allowed him to entertain the advent of Self as a possible consequence of his sufferings. This brilliant concept was even more effective because it had come from his own inner struggle to heal. Through the practice of spiritual vision and mental reframing, he was able to see that his healing was in owning, expressing, and releasing old emotions, mental constructs, and expectations that no longer served him. The lens of spiritual vision transformed his apparent mistakes, failures, and shortcomings into doorways to positive movement away from fear. He soon came to see that his misperceived shortcomings were just signs of his potential emerging. As time went on, he knew he would have to stay observant of his tendency to judge himself harshly or wallow in self-pity if he was to see his potential both spiritually and personally unfold. One day he said he was unmotivated in school, which was a repeat of a pattern he'd experienced in his youth. He was able to eventually remember that he had previously been a great student. He was now suffering and even lying about his grades to convince his parents they were not wasting their money on his college tuition. The remembrance of his previous level of potential called him to change his behavior. Within one semester, he turned his grades around and felt smart and honest again.

As we venture further into the integration of this motivational technology, we notice that we can heal our self-reproach in chunks. By seeing problems as gateways to change and seeing mistakes as opportunities to grow, we remind ourselves to always ask, "What am I learning?" Suffering can create curiosity, and curiosity can ignite the willingness to go beyond to places we need to travel if we're to be transformed. As I progressed on the spiritual ladder of awareness, I relied less on ritual and formalized religious practice. I still went to them periodically as tools and viable options to navigate certain lessons but not in such a fearful, clinging way. I grew up doing things to feel good. I undid any mistake with good deeds and protected against any fear by buying safety and creating safe barriers to maintain a fragile inner integrity. I "did to be," because when I went inside to pull from my bank account of being, I got memories of only a few shreds of previous doings that somehow met the grade and could be counted on to give me a short-lived boost. At one point, I noticed that I would read all my army medals, college awards, and write-ups and stare at my graduate diploma in order to feel better on a tough day. I was constantly overlooking that the person who'd accomplished those things had never left and was always present. I soon realized I was searching for something more certain and more solid, something that could only be found on a more essential level and beyond what I could have created or changed. I began to see the concept of being as I did my nationality. I'm Irish and Italian. I am those things no matter what I do. My DNA will always be the same, no matter what clothes I wear or what I say. When I understood this truth, I saw my pursuit of Self in a different light. This led me to kick back and observe.

If Self lives in oneness and exists in a state beyond duality, then it must fully integrate doing and being and make the result something else entirely. An analogy that comes to mind is the union of hydrogen and oxygen to beget water. The effect is a jump in structure, but the original elements are maintained. The human journey has several rules that can't be avoided if one is attempting to evolve. It incorporates finiteness, which is about time, process, measurable growth, separation, boundaries, achievement, and completion. These are all I am not. As a spiritual being, I live in the infiniteness of the eternal now and only live using resonance, unity, expansiveness, and oneness. On a spiritual level, these expressions are my lineage and have divine grace as their cohort.

To move to a concept that I've been breaching thus far but that needs clarity now, we have to address the thought of mistakes or what used to be referred to as *sin*. The realization of the illusion of sin became clear through the lens of spiritual vision. Using the healing miracle thought stream *We never really do anything wrong; we just make mistakes out of ignorance*, we have and will do things that lead down dark side roads. Eventually, all side roads can lead to transformation. This mistake-forgiveness process has one of the greatest outcomes. Compassion is born out of the integration of conditional and unconditional love. Imagine one of the greatest tools of evolution on a spiritual level being an integration of our worst and best endeavors and our finite and infinite nature. This felt much better to resonate with than a nonstop shame-and-guilt vibration.

The past is best used as a measurement system to adjust in the now. Shame, guilt, regret, and all other dark teachers in the emotional body are perfect for their mission, as they alert us to what needs to be observed and changed, but they aren't to be overused or made into solid states of mind that limit us. Such limitation is prevalent in many seekers and less spiritually minded people due to the amount of culturally reinforced guilt and punishment in the media and in dysfunctional relationships. Life unfolds in miraculous ways when we recognize dark emotions as teachers. These teachers help us learn about who we aren't and point us to where we can hear divine guidance more clearly. When I respond in harmony to what is in front of me with the intention to embrace and learn more, truth illuminates, and peace surrounds.

What would compel you to aspire to find inner peace but the knowledge of it and what it isn't? When I respond to what is in front of me with the intent to change the situation, I'm acting out of impulses generated from dark emotions, assuming what's happening is bad or painful rather than trusting that it is divine will and being patient as the lesson unfolds. When I act out of my own perception and don't use contemplation, true neutrality, surrender, and patience, any divine expression becomes blocked. I'm left to fix the problem on the natural-mind level. This grows tedious and steals my peace. My whole journey then becomes a challenge to stay centered in Self and surrender to what is in front of me to handle. This can be a place of movement and growth but often requires intense effort. Happily, though, as I continue to practice, I'm able to feel and express more Self-love. As time pushed me forward, I discovered there was a divine purpose in the school of earth that I could hold on to and teach.

From the natural-mind perspective, life is a battleground of winning and losing, all enacted in the search for personal definition. In fact, the more you lose on earth, the greater your personal strides can become spiritually as you learn more about who you aren't. When we begin to awaken as spiritual beings, self-love and forgiveness become our immediate and constant companions. We can also become instruments for the awakening of others. This allows our mistakes to become welcomed teachers. Recovering from mistakes' undoing is part of the sacredness of the journey, not something to fear. As we move through the transparencies of what we aren't, our Self can make its grand entrance, and our conscious contact with our particular higher power grows. When we see what we really are not, we awaken to a peace that has no end. We can then use the past as a measurement tool and a system for being in the now by constantly using divinely inspired choices. When we bless everything, especially our houses, food, meditations, friends, and enemies, it becomes sacred. Our Self is found in the vibrancy of the interaction of what is and what isn't, what works and what doesn't work, and what we can see and what's still hidden. We can always use our experience and the ability to feel the grace found therein. But this journey of faith calls for a courageous heart. We also get a chance to glimpse oneness when we see the Self as a collective level of consciousness that includes all others. On earth, this is often a completely new experience.

If we want to know who we are, then we must pay attention to all experiences primarily through the tool of humility. We must understand that awakening also constitutes a loss of a personal identity and all that was defined as identity up until that point—in short, "all I am not." What is not creates desire and sets in motion our passion to find our Self.

Unless we agree to suffer we cannot be free of suffering.
—D. T. Suzuki

CHAPTER 10
SELF VERSUS PERSONAL SELF

The poor farmer makes weeds; the mediocre farmer makes crops; the skilled farmer makes fertile soil.
—Zen saying

In the Self, the self is lost. The lost personal and body self is the treasure. The concept of personal self and natural mind versus Self and divine mind brings to light the ultimate in dualities' ability to bring clarity. If the primary purpose of this world is to teach that we are much more than anything that has to do with death or limits, then limits are perfect in their ability to remind us of our unlimited potential. The human heart beats to a finite cadence. The spiritual heart beats to an infinite cadence. When the physical heart skips or adds a beat, there is concern. When the spiritual heart skips or adds a beat, there is growth. You stop where you are and feel revelations as the new territory comes into view. There is elation in the infiniteness.

The beauty of this tool is that it, like all other spiritual technologies, works in a world of paradox and limitations. This new territory gives us respite from the linearity of time as we evolve at our own pace, experiencing the full range of our mortality and divinity. We need a body to realize we are spirits. The same is true with the personality self and its divine origin, Self. As the eternal Self, we first create a personal self limited by mortality and perception plagued with physical pain, character flaws, and misperceptions to prompt the journey to evolve. Denying human persona or natural mind is like denying the train we're traveling on to get to a destination. Without its specific purpose, our human meaning remains status quo. Though it is confusing in the beginning, through this use of contrast, we become clearer as to what our spiritual path and subsequent missions are. When we deny our humanness or spirituality, confusion is the only result. The miracle in this is that by seeing things differently and with added clarity, we can shed unneeded traits and fear-filled perceptions with more skill. There is no escape from the world we see through human eyes and experience through the natural mind while only identifying our life through perception while in a body. Once we embrace this truth, we can activate the courageous willingness inherent in Self to realize that the personal self was always a prison with an open door.

You are always finite and infinite in your life on earth. You inhale and exhale. This is how duality teaches. You are more infinite than finite, but you walk the finite path until it ends. There is no bypassing it; one must always graduate to exit. Finitude is the in breath. Infinity is the out breath. What we are never changes, but who we are changes constantly. In order to realize the power inherent in this dualistic interplay, we must understand the lessons taught when we incarnate into a world perceived as a realm of separation. There is really no personal self, but we use its character like a set of clothing in order to live in this world. This is due to the premise that all that is real is unchangeable. The Self is always available to inform and direct, as it knows the mission intimately. The divine mind can rarely be heard above the emotional roar of natural-mind thought, and as a result, most people cannot hear or recognize its wisdom. It's as if we have an all-knowing, gentle guide with us as we live out our daily lives, but we rarely do what it takes to make the communication clearer and more practical. The tools in this manual are specifically designed to bring this subtle voice to light.

True wisdom can lead the way, as this voice of divine love awaits as an abiding presence in Self. Many seekers access this wisdom through the practices of meditation, contemplation, reading, dream interpretation, journaling, and spiritual counseling. The primary goal of the Self is to accomplish any soul mission chosen for spiritual evolution while on earth. These soul missions are designed to move us forward on the soul level to a place where there is only knowing, not perception. We might even find that in time, our level of consciousness increases, bringing with it more peace, love, and joy. From living with a natural mind, we learn much about how to be successful while in a body, but Self, with its access to divine mind and connection to wisdom, can open to a level of knowingness that will never be satisfied with finite endeavors and outcomes. These earth missions can bring great pain or pleasure and are designed to use time as a way to slow down learning lessons as we continue to develop abilities, such as spiritual vision, divine listening, and compassion. These Self-generated mindsets await our use of the vortex of tools to bring to light the divine inheritance uniquely designed for each soul.

As the personal self feels its limits, curiosity grows. This self then becomes more willing to use spiritual tools. In contrast, Self is in direct communication with the divine and constantly assists our evolution through many channels of grace to save time and bring light. The Self knows no boundaries, and it is not limited by perceptions or distortions. There are no obstacles for the Self to hurdle, except for the ripeness of its human sidekick—natural mind and personal self—to believe and hear the messages. The thoughts generated from divine mind help us to make better personal choices, because it sees reality without distortion. The Self has the wonderful ability to hear divine guidance clearly, and once coupled with the desire and skills to repeat wisdom clearly to the personal self and to extend it to others in verbal, written word, or practice, it becomes a powerful teacher on earth. As we become more aware of our own divinity, we realize that the source of all our love and joy comes from this transformation.

The Self can go by many names and be felt in many ways. Some people refer to Self as our soul, the Holy Spirit, Jesus, Krishna, an advanced saint, an ascended master, or a teacher. It also is clear that because Self has no limits, we must all be part of its potential, whether we recognize it or not. Others liken the Self to wise-mindedness or a fully actualized intellect or genius. Some say it's divine truth or wisdom. No matter the name, the greatest distinguishing character is that we are not the author of its truth, wisdom, or love. These gifts flow through us and extend into the world for a greater good.

From this level, communication comes from knowingness and not a situation of learning, as the personal self does. The concept of having a working sidekick self that has a personality and a separate body and a Self already in place makes life vibrant and clearly shows us the power and blessing of having free will. Clarity becomes the primary lesson as we learn more about how to discern between different aspects of the selves. A main concept in this book is the full embodiment and movement into Self as a conscious experience. To become less you and all you is the goal for many seekers. It becomes apparent that in the absence of definitions, or solid concepts, the Self is actually beyond definitions.

Life in personal self is still a gift, but once we experience the Self and its inherent peace and joy, we can see life as the gift it is intended to be. When you use spiritual tools, such as the neutral witness and meditation, and pay attention without worrying about how this *you* is doing, the movement of awakening becomes possible. Without this clarity, our alignment with and pursuit of truths can cause confusion.

As I learned more truth and became more adept in the use of humility, it became clear that a large amount of fear resides in our subconscious. The dualistic interplay between different aspects of the selves can heal low self-esteem as we allow for divine thoughts to increase awareness of our innate innocence and hold our worthiness firmly in place. The natural mind constantly runs programs that are misguided and self-castigating. It also is apparent that we are addicted in some way to negative thoughts about self. This dynamic is created by the natural mind's mandate for fear and its attempt to keep us vigilant to aspects of personality that can create the worst outcomes, in order to stimulate awareness and avoid the things that cause pain and death. To complicate matters, in the absence of clarity, the truth you align with could be your own truth, not the absolute or sacred truth. Without clarity, the lens you see through shows you only what you can best bring into focus in the murky field of vision and perception you have. We must always watch the part of self that says, "This is the way it should be done." The energy that gives power to the body is the need for fulfillment and protection, but without the ability to know truth from falsehood, we can often be misguided. The guardian of the personal self is the natural mind, and because its assignment is to seek pleasure and avoid pain, when it loses clarity, even this pursuit can lead to death. Many lost souls choose suicide or drug addiction in an attempt to avoid pain but wind up dying in this world of inner fear and avoidance.

Complicating things more, we often judge our personal worth on the outcome of endeavors and the words and behaviors of others who are lacking or incapable of allowing success or giving love. The fear and sense of lack that fuel this energy source push the development and utilization of natural talents and pursuits into areas that could be nebulous, unclear, or dangerous. The natural mind often picks one path to follow, and it assures itself that this path is the one and only path to take because it serves personal-self aspirations. There are times when the personal self, through its natural mind, chooses through so-called spiritual eyes; loses touch with clarity; and becomes its own higher power. When this occurs, the lesson is to integrate the dualistic and karmic lessons of different aspects of the selves, trusting in and surrendering to the direction best suited to meet your soul mission. Until we bypass this confusing mess of the natural-mind-powered, obscure voice, we won't break the bonds and chains of attachment to poorly conceived concepts.

If we truly want to live the reality of Self, then we must be conscious to the present experience in the eternal now. The neutral observation of either self from any angle without identification with the body is an invitation for the Self to enter. Awareness empowered by our intention to evolve will keep moving us forward to the inheritance found in our spiritual evolution. Seeing things from above the battlefield is the key. Our eternally preexisting divinity is all-inclusive and, if fostered and made present in Self, will affect every part of life. Keep in mind that the goal is freedom—until it dawns on you that you are already free. This freedom is not something in the distant future to be earned by painful efforts. It is eternally one's own and at the ready to be used.

It might appear we are beating the natural mind, with all its preprogrammed thoughts and winning freedom, but all we are ever doing on the level of intellect is constantly reinforcing that we can never escape from perception's grasp. There is no winning over death, because there is no death of Self; there is only a divine transfer of consciousness. Liberation is not an acquisition. It is a matter of courage—the courage found in both heart and minds to believe you are free already. Act on it. Once the shift occurs to Self, the loss of devotion to personality and natural mind is not a result of decision or work. You will no longer be interested in its circuitous route to nowhere. This is where acting as if works best. Your Self can help your personality become your saintly self if that's your path; it's just waiting for your full permission and whole belief in its welcome. Daily thought takes the form of a need-minded voice in an impulse-first mechanism called thinking. This natural-mind mechanism, with all its symbols and identifications, longs for the attachments that give it value and safety. This personal self is never able to live in certainty, because perceptions of these things can change. In contrast, Self is the doorway to certainty and invulnerability and is accessed through faith.

The following descriptions of the personal self are designed to help with discernment between the personal self and the Self. This list is designed not to point out greater or lesser but to give more clarity as to the equally important roles of Self and self in our evolution.

- The personal self will imbibe in wasteful indulgences.

- The personal self will repeat mistakes to define its boundaries and make itself unique.
- The personal self has many opinions.
- The personal self creates community through suffering.
- The personal self separates rather than binding.
- The personal self sets aside without learning the lesson.
- The personal self does not trust in the divine impulse.
- The personal self is constantly learning and feels lack.

Through compassion, we sing praises to those who falter. We become aware that they have hit a wall and know where the edge of the lesson is for them. We realize that their stuck point can actually awaken a stronger contrasting desire in us to search for the divine source with a clearer intent. As long as you think your personal self is the real you, your Self will seem like the sidekick, the fantasy partner, or the spiritual you. Switching this dynamic is the real healing in these tools. We become tired of their circuitous routes. Through pointed intention into newness, we move to welcome the Self through contemplation, awareness, and other devices of surrender.

The following abilities become accessible as our new belief unlocks their gifts. First and foremost, the Self does not have to strive for safety in a world that constantly changes. It only sees the world as a classroom for forgiveness and remembrance of oneness. The personal self is activated by the pursuit of safety, and it will manipulate for love. When it thinks it is loved, it feels safe. The Self is unconditional love, and even though the present lesson might look and feel like hell, Self always recalls the best lessons to assess the current situation. The Self does not move with the outside world of good or bad, happy or sad. It knows it is truth beyond thought, yet it is thinking.

The real need all of us have—and a main purpose of this book—is to bring seekers to a self-state that is solid. This can only be experienced once Self is in place. This divine condition exists with a love that has no conditions and lives with a certainty that knows how to deal with all conditions through a deep realization of the truth of its being. This is the place where you can access the peace beyond recognition. It is our destiny to know who we are in loving glory without demanding recognition of any kind. Journeying with both selves teaches us who we really are and who we do not want to be.

The personal self lives with a body voice that constantly critiques our lives. These thoughts can create much pain, as they trigger the core of our victimhood default and the tendency for self-punishment. We eventually have to release the blame by projecting this pain onto an internal aspect, which can deplete our self-esteem, or an external entity or sacred other.

What if we never do anything wrong? What if the earth is a perfect school of forgiveness and learning, and we do things that lead us down dark roads only because that gives us the best chance to learn? Self does not have the distortion or the boundaries of personal self. It is all-inclusive, yet it comes from a perfectly unique perspective. All things are possible when we live in Self through the study of and devotion to spiritual tools, such as the law of attraction. Self holds everything in wisdom, so all things are understood through spiritual vision. This unlocks the divine underbelly of what is in front of us at the moment. It is like living in the same neighborhood for fifty years. You will know your way around. There is no more learning, because everything is understood. The Self resides in complete harmony with the divine. There are no more obstacles.

The Self can inform the personal self as we open our decision-making minds through true neutrality and listening. Divine love experienced as wisdom is the water running through the pipe of this gift of Self. This integration of natural mind and divine mind is a soul expression that gives us vibrancy. It is not perfection, because perfection on earth is subjective; it is a life with sacred energy and grace. The openness of heart and mind we create must be free of judgment and clear of personal-self agenda. When wisdom is received, it is trusted. This will allow it to manifest in our lives. Self is like a big brother or sister who knows the ropes and tries to care for an aspect of the natural mind (intellect) that still holds hollowness, insecurity, and fear.

The following are concepts that will bring us closer to living in Self:

- Acknowledge our concerns, feelings, and conditions that our present self is not giving us to bring fulfillment.
- Do our best to find peace with what is at present, remembering it is still part of a holy evolution.
- Apply our best human wisdom.
- Follow our joy.
- Imagine the hollowness felt (as we let go of personal self) in the emptiness of surrender.
- Pay attention between hollowness and the fertile emptiness of surrender.
- Listen for either self in the emptiness.
- Realize hollowness is a less-than-open state, and emptiness opens us up for receptivity.

In conclusion, once we allow the Self to run the show, we won't forget the personal self and body; we just won't be as identified with them. Once we see the personal self clearly, we can carry it around like a pet. We will no longer need to have the pride of authorship the personal self craves. We will feel beauty in all of creation and gratitude for the experience to have incarnated.

The analogy that best describes the difference in the selves and the process of spiritual evolution is the story of Michelangelo. He saw a huge piece of marble in a quarry one day, and he immediately envisioned *David*. The unfinished stone is the personal self, with all its rough edges and mistakes. *David* is the perfect product already existing in the stone's potential. Michelangelo chipped away at what was not needed to get to the essence and core of divinity inherent in the *David* in us all. You must imagine yourself as an actor who plays a character in an earth suit, but that's not the real you. We are only doorways of essence. The Self awaits your total belief, just as the *David* awaited its release. Your ability to integrate humanness and divinity with a new love contains great power and potential. This potential can be startling at times and will show itself in many ways or not show at all but still be active. In duality, we will still be without certainty at times. Desires will take over. On the path to Self, time slows things down enough to allow for unfolding. We can learn slowly, take in the lessons, and extend them later. Personal characteristics can be put under the care of the natural mind, but they are powered by an evolutionary energy coming from the body's life force. One can accomplish much with his or her human learning and imagination, but it will all end. In contrast, Self creates through extension of divinity itself, and our unique souls animate it. The personal self is run by fear, lack, and the need to define itself. Even through success or earth fulfillment, we can only glimpse true accomplishment and permanence. The Self is whole and an expression of the divine source of all essential life as our conscious soul. Each soul's extension in this level of higher consciousness looks different in its manifestation on earth. For many, a minideath is to come, and a minibirth is to follow.

> Behold I do not give lectures with a little charity. When I give, I give from myself.
> —Walt Whitman

CHAPTER 11
FORGIVENESS

One forgives to the degree that one loves.
—**Francois de La Rochefoucauld**

There are many ways of looking at life. One such conception focuses on seeing that our personal self, with its host body, and spirit Self are separated in ways that are irreconcilable. In this vision, we are aware of more separation than union, and as this mindset grows stronger, we will see everything and everyone in separation everywhere. One of the most limiting concepts of separation is the belief that God is elsewhere and that we can find the place in which it presides only through extreme devotion and much hard work.

This separatist view, when used as a way to live, creates a world where differentness and diversity are rewarded. This mindset is then constantly reinforced by culture and daily experience and becomes the default perceptive lens of the human eye. This dynamic is best described as "We see only what we are looking for." This can be a cause of prejudice, hatred, negative projection, and revenge. We naturally feel unsafe in this world because of our identification with the fragility of the body. We sensationalize the roots of the fear-based, inherent natural-mind survival tool and highlight the inherent violence and mistakes humankind has made in the past. When there is an absence of forgiveness and gratitude in this mindset, the earth school can be seen through a lens of constant fear. This type of belief system automatically assumes that something or someone is wrong. When we live with this vision as our primary lens, we see the root of man's inhumanity to man. By becoming aware of this thought stream, we can uncover our intolerance of things, people, values, beliefs, and anything else that helps reinforce a personal self that needs to define itself on a primary and solitary level based on drama, conflict, and opposition. The issues that create thoughts of separation run much deeper in our unconscious than most are aware.

We've always needed to discern danger and threat, but when we judge each other's beliefs or ways of life, we can create a destructive loneliness that leads down dark paths. This is not a statement about values; it is a restatement of the inherent intolerance built into the natural mind. On a primitive level of consciousness, discernment of safety and the intention of strangers were needed observations in our primordial strivings. This evolutionary quality works well in a world that believes in separation and awaits attack. As perception constantly reinforces itself for personal validation, the concept of separation gets recharged on unconscious and conscious levels frequently. This cloudy premise projected from a subconscious fear that feels as though we are awaiting punishment for doing something wrong at some point long past and can be seen as depicted and reinforced in our creation myths. This is the basic premise on which the perfect dualistic counterpart for the sacred remedy of forgiveness is best applied. The correction for the unforgiveness mindset is to shift from this heavier, pain-filled vision fueled by guilty projections to a vision inspired by the Self and its grace-filled visage. The word for this is simply *forgiveness*. When we forgive on any level, we allow it to be known that somewhere in our hearts, we no longer choose separation. We return to the natural spiritual state of unity consciousness. When we look at our lives through the mindset of forgiveness, we begin to heal. When we carry this mindset as our conscious centering, we can extend throughout the world. Even if we still feel victimized, the movement to forgive gives permission to feel truth with greater clarity and humility and scale the ladder of life with kindness.

At the top of this forgiveness ladder is the divine belief behind the premise of this book: we are all innocent. All that occurs, even in our ignorance and mistakes, is divinely inspired, supported, and designed to help us evolve on a soul level. When we use forgiveness, we are touched with grace to resolve a problem or heal a relationship in real time.

One important note about all spiritual technology is that any tool we use is not ours to own. We are not the authors of any of it. There is no one forgiving another, and no country is forgiving another. That would bring such a divinely inspired tool back down into the finite world to be used by personalities to reinforce separation and further confirm their elitism. Anytime we make a decision from the Self, we call in a divine principle to help heal and create conditions for miracles and grace. Upon realizing Self is not a finite presence and does not take a sense of pride from claiming authorship in performing a personal action, we can feel a deeper peace.

On the lowest levels of the forgiveness ladder, we believe we are forgiving another. On that level, to be forgiving and of a forgiving mind would contribute to the density of our prideful presence because we would or could take credit. When we do so, the only reward is found in a fleeting emotional boost. In contrast, when we have gratitude for being only a device in the use of divine tools, peace and soul evolution are the rewards. We must be willing to hold all apparently hurtful intentions, words, and actions as a sacred challenge to practice these enablers until we are transformed.

The Self includes all and forgives by shining an illuminated and quintessential light of understanding that includes and empowers everything as a divine teacher. This is because it sources from a wisdom beyond perception. This Self knows and orchestrates the inherent purpose behind all soul-inspired experiences because of their direct connection. To begin to understand forgiveness is to be introduced to divine flexibility at its best. We can shift from holding another responsible and playing judge to seeing innocence. We come to this conclusion as we believe that the personal self lives in limitation and often makes choices as a result of an arrogance-driven, misguided perception. With surrender, we can start with the belief that we are a victim and forgive an attacker or withholder. This style initiates a dialogue of forgiveness that can lead to compassion and empathy. One can see an incident as a lesson and forgive because it serves a good purpose.

In a job I once had, a stoic man would not say hello to me or acknowledge my presence at all. We passed by each other in the clinic dozens of times daily. I originally hated and judged him. I labeled him every name in the book until I realized he was a great teacher of unconditional love. I even tricked my ego to give him permission not to like me and not to see me, even though everything in me screamed judgment at him relentlessly. Using a forgiveness mind that knew everything was divinely inspired. I recognized that he was one of the dark teachers I'd asked for when I decided to become a spiritual teacher on earth. He reminded me that the way we think of others determines how we ultimately feel about ourselves and vice versa. I was being shown that I needed to forgive my own unfriendliness and coldness, even though my overzealous natural mind likely told me I was much more blessed. I had projected an unwanted personal-self aspect onto someone else. *Perhaps I am not as holy as my natural mind would lead me to believe*, I thought, *as I am still attracting these teachers and lessons.*

To grow in the awareness and power of the forgiveness mind means I truly accept that we can be attacked at any time, and the attacks are perfect as instructors. As I evolve, it becomes harder to feel my hatred or anger and immediately retaliate. Many seekers will first grapple with this concept, but once we accept our demons in order to overcome them, learning can commence faster and more efficiently. As I was filled with more faith, I could do deeper self-searching and healing and soon began putting on a forgiveness mind more quickly. Spiritual seekers will probably struggle with the aforementioned concept that negative experiences are powerful teachers, but through surrender, humility, and the neutral witness, we can get enough distance to see how all spiritual tools ultimately serve to make our lives better.

I continued to watch with neutral eyes that were still invested in seeing and feeling clearly and harmlessly. It is an act of arrogance to remain a spiritual seeker judging the path of others, pitying them, or blessing them from a distant pulpit of personal self. I often fell into this natural-mind trick and used my spirituality to hide from the depth of my human lessons. I specifically recall using the arrogant belief that I was above others because I had the way.

I often forgot to forgive my personal self, and in doing so, I forgot to allow compassion for other humans feeling the pain of this world. How else was I going to remember my own inner child, who is prone to being wounded? In the beginning, I let go of anger from every angle I could because I had low self-esteem and feared rejection. I was buying safety from feelings I felt were intolerable and had dire consequences. As a result of this practice, I am now able to integrate my human needs to feel hurt, anger, and resentment with spiritual truth, which allows me to see that these negative feelings too are teachers, not attackers. When we abide in the mind of forgiveness, we must eventually discern how to stay safe socially while letting go of the tendency to accumulate resentments. This takes time and leaves us vulnerable. During this stage, we must have courageous hearts and trust the process. We also become more adept at letting go and forgetting past hurts and wounds but not forgetting their lessons. As I progressed in my understanding of forgiveness through practice and trust, I realized verbal attacks from others provided opportunities for patience as well. Salvation showed itself as the undoing of an aspect of the personal self that lives intolerantly as a choice maker. Being allegedly attacked over and over again without retaliation can actually loosen this fear-based natural tendency to protect a self that takes itself too seriously. Once we see attack and slights as opportunities to evolve, our social life is transformed, and we can then see that joy and love are its welcome gifts and can make places, occurrences, and people holy again.

Forgiveness has many levels within its healing structure. We can forgive an object or situation, such as a person or an injury. We can forgive the intention for an attack, slight, or oversight. We can forgive ignorance and write it off as fate or chance. We must eventually accept the wound and forgive the natural mind for even having the perception of being wounded. The trick to healing by using this divine tool is to forgive it all. Every layer must be whitewashed with a new story. You must let go of all weaponry.

When I refer to *weaponry*, I mean attacking thoughts either past or present and all forms of retaliatory plans or actions held in mind or previously held in mind as well as negative judgments. Lessons have no relevance if we carry the battle in our mind and await a new symbol with which to fight. In some cases, this can attract a new adversary, which forces us to start over again. We must always finish a soul curriculum as we integrate it and transform from it. Forgiveness is the bridge to true healing. True healing is not always seen in forgetting, but it can encompass a compassionate view of the person, event, or self-action that allows for the full complement of understanding and transformation to occur. To understand and to release the pain of unforgiveness, we must forgive all things. Once we understand this, integration can occur. This is the formula for evolution or transformation.

In the case of the victim–abuser scenario, it is important that neither one remains in the role of good or evil. When you trust the lesson of your attacker, you give more trust to yourself. You gain back the Self- and self-love that was lost as victim or abuser. To be victims is to diminish ourselves, despite the popular belief in powerlessness. Famous accounts of abuse have created courageousness and soul expressions of light. A good example of this can be found in Viktor Frankl's *Man's Search for Meaning*.

The process of learning forgiveness through relationships can be confusing. It is especially hard for spiritually based thinkers with good intentions and strong wills to forgive on deeper levels and remain clear about how to proceed in relationships. We cannot tolerate repeated abusive behavior when we are listening to our wisdom minds and seeing things from the witness viewpoint. We can always attach prayer and compassion, but there will be times when we must move on or let go of a toxic person. This person no longer serves the divine purpose, and it is our mission to navigate out of the drama. To forgive is to move out of the part of the natural mind that craves conflict and creates drama. Even when we feel the fear that immobilizes us and have no clue how to resolve the social issues between people, we can forgive by changing our perspectives about them. Any heavy thoughts we carry about others weigh us down, reinforce our own hatred of the personal self, and obscure the Self from operating in our daily lives.

Another hint that helps with forgiveness is the understanding of time. If a trauma or slight is in the past and we are feeling it now, then we are carrying it into the present because the lesson or hidden teaching hasn't been learned yet. We are always living in the eternal now.

Do not forget to rest in the deep silence of Self when you need clarity or a thought that works. You and everyone else were created innocent before donning the natural mind and personal self. To carry guilt is to build it up, no matter how long ago the guilt was born. Guilt can help us live productive lives on earth when we use it as a situational guide, but when it becomes a state of mind, we become dangerous to ourselves and others. If we are always doing our best in the eyes of the divine, despite natural-mind programming, we can never do anything sinful or wrong. We will make mistakes and wander down dark roads, but choosing forgiveness as a travel companion can rectify those mistakes. No one has sinned; we are all just called to learn.

> The fragrance of the violet sheds its scent
> on the heel that crushed it.
> —Mark Twain

CHAPTER 12
JOY

I am coming to believe that our source wills us to have joy as a regular experience in our lives. It is the marrow of love in its purest form. Pure love has no fear, and without fear, joy can shine through. It is humankind's purpose and valuable option to be living examples of joy on earth.

When I recognized my mission as a healer, I began teaching with contagious joy and watched it pull people to my words. I had begun my healership in a deep depression as a young man and vowed to find a lasting joy in which to live. As I experienced the energy of joy more frequently, I began to believe that joy could actually be a pursuit and that it had a healing energy of its own. I began to look at joy as a spiritual tool. Prior to that revelation, I'd concluded joy was just one of many human feelings, like happiness, contentment, and excitement. As my relationship with this nondualistic mindset unfolded, I realized it was not earned but was always part of Self, waiting to be experienced once the conditions were right. Happiness has unhappiness, contentment has discontentment, and excitement has dullness. Joy is its own gift.

In my role as a teacher of spiritual technology, I feel compelled to bring joy in its authenticity through my actions, words, and daily life. It's like a recruitment poster for the spiritual journey. No one wants to follow a sullen seeker or teacher. Joy shows itself as an attribute of love that can extend a sacred invitation to follow. It is also a harbinger of the peace we all long for. Joy, as love, is our inheritance as divine beings, and this precious condition is our buried treasure when we do the work to summon Self.

Joy is an aspect of sacred love. It is the original state of being on the soul level in the same way nationality is on the physical level. The soul is pure joy at the essence level, but it is rarely experienced or held on to, because the concept of Self is filtered through misconception, pain, trauma, and lack. We call this *the past*. Some lives are actually tortuous, and even though this can set the table for joy in a dualistic turnaround, these tortuous lives seem hopeless and joyless. This misperception of the natural mind most often blocks the free flow of joy in our lives. Joy cannot be altered, but it can be controlled or squelched in extreme conditions by our allowing negative thought streams to rule the natural mind. Victimhood, revenge, and shame-based and guilt-based self-attacks are just a few of the thoughts that squelch joy's loving presence.

Joy is an everlasting and infinitely sourced divine expression. It is universal and timeless, much like unconditional love. This love is the origin of all love, but the natural mind uses it conditionally to accomplish personal needs and wants. Joy can be suppressed, but it can bubble forth or burst out of its containment in any circumstance. We don't create joy; it is a gift of Self as it flows through our lives. Once we awaken to its beauty, we can welcome it by making our divine minds fertile ground for its reception. This is the purpose and payoff of using the spiritual technology espoused in this book. Each mindset, ritual, and revelation serves as fertilizer for holding joy, peace, and love more consistently. At some point, everyone can experience joy and respond with a smile or humor. This concept is represented in Mary Shelley's *Frankenstein* when the monster smiles after being handed a daisy by a child. The human spirit is joy and can return to itself. It is ultimately part of our spiritual DNA, but only we can allow the experience of joy to be felt. Since it is our natural state on a spiritual level, its presence pulls us vibrationally higher and calls forth Self with more desire. Joy is what red blood cells are to blood and is the essence of divine love.

To understand that joy has no dualistic opposite is to realize its power. It never becomes mitigated and only brings safety as it flows like warm morning light into the most hidden recesses of life. This light can travel unfettered around corners, underground, through water, and into the epicenter of life. When expressed, joy washes through and over us, affecting everything and everyone it touches. The touch of joy is uplifting, as it inspires and enriches. One can choose to receive joy or not. Happiness is earned from an activity fulfilled, but joy is felt once we are aligned and appreciative of any outcome or unfulfilment. Gratitude summons joy like no other tool and allows for its greatest experience. This is because of its ability to be used without conditions. We can be thankful for light or dark outcomes. Joy is our gift for being awake enough to see that the journey is divine in itself.

Not received, joy travels on. Unhappiness may be felt. Stasis will continue, and hope will not grow, but joy can feed hope like no other emotion as its vibration germinates its seeds as they await stimulation. One can choose to receive joy, and it can be felt in any way the individual allows: happiness, bliss, peace, deep quiet, or joy. Its receipt prompts movement and the blossoming of any positive inspiration. Life runs on no matter what the individual chooses, and this is divinely inspired. The spark that brings forth our life is chosen on the soul level, but our daily choices bring the lessons that paint the canvas of the daily happenstance of our lives. There is no choice more wise or meaningful than the one that best serves. Joy, depression, and suffering are all choices. If all choices are ultimately held and inspired by our desire to evolve and are designed to teach and help in our evolution while we're on earth, then even pain-filled choices that create suffering and can be understood only in contrast are also divine helpers. These powerful dark teachers can pave the way for the acceptance of joy.

Embracing joy is a matter of personal preference. This does not mean unhappiness is always the person's preference. Unhappiness can be a default setting in a life that brings forth suffering, but it is always meant to be healed. The opposite of happiness is unhappiness, but there is no opposite of joy. It is an expression of a divine principle that infers there is no opposite of light; its absence is simply darkness. Similarly, there is no opposite of heat; its absence is cold. When we center ourselves and observe the full expression of *what is* brought to our lives in the moment, we can be the light of joy in its purity. On days when we are scattered and misaligned, we are still the light of joy but not its purity. Even when we choose to follow joy or suffering, we have available the options to choose to vibrantly express all the gray areas in between. Welcome to the sacred experience of the earth school.

The precious light of joy is especially clear when we are in easy, open relationships with all that is. We trust that everything and everyone in our lives is divinely inspired and sent. As spiritual seekers, we can choose to bring joy deep inside our beingness. It can be perfectly expressed out of the baseline of who we are. When we are operating in our most desired, vibrant way, joy can manifest at its best as infinite kindness and compassion for everyone we meet. When this is our daily intent and the conditions are right, others can be awakened and stirred as our joy extends outward. They often want to mimic our intention as joy calls them to align with itself. If the soul expression, which can be seen in a thought, action, or activity, does not call them to alignment, they might find our joy-filled soul expression uncomfortable and find themselves repulsed. I saw and felt this first while running a group. I was resonating with clear, compassionate, healing energy, when out of nowhere, a member began to have chest pains. I had to get a nurse to tend to the body. He eventually returned, saying only that he had felt warm energy surrounding his heart, which had become uncomfortable.

Many people are either not aware of spiritual work or defiantly against it. I eventually learned to be vigilant as to the readiness of people's receptivity when extending healing love and found that the negative reactivity happened less and less. When we are not joyful, we are not hurting anyone but are not able to share joy. Joy is a powerful tool that can affect others in a number of ways, as do the other technologies in this book.

The many experiences of joy have expressed their healing power in my life over the years in the following ways:

1. Joy clears the mental palate, allowing decisions to be made that serve the highest good.
2. Joy clears the emotional palate, allowing states of being that serve the highest good.

3. Joy clears the spiritual palate, allowing the soul to clearly express what it needs for fulfillment to be felt.
4. Joy is a way and a meaningful choice, but be cautious. To believe joy can be or should be experienced in everyone's life is arrogant and ignorant.
5. Being around animals and children or doing pastimes that are purposeful or meaningful can also serve to increase your vibration of joy.
6. Joy serves all humanity by bringing peace into the world. The soul calls for what it needs. When it feels fulfilled, there is joy, no matter what it has called for.

The following personal declarations awaken inner joy:

1. I awaken the Self-love gifted to me, intending for it to fill my energy field and my life in ways greater and deeper than I have ever experienced.
2. The inner joy embedded within Self-love greets me.
3. A smile rises up from within me and fills my life. I feel filled to overflowing.
4. I allow my inner joy to guide me.
5. I am the joy I feel.
6. I hope joy and love are with us often.

Some others, even though they are living what appear to be prosperous and functional lives for their specific soul missions and evolution, might have completely different views. The things we do as seekers to learn on earth might seem tedious, but the body's limited and fleeting capacity to hold joy can be felt and used to build the courage to become a more potent messenger of this divine gift. Once we become more familiar with joy's vibration, it can give our activities and intentions extra energy for manifestation, which naturally will remove all obstacles to healing.

> Joy is the meaning and purpose of life, the whole aim and end of existence.
> —Aristotle

CHAPTER 13
COURAGEOUS HEART

Courage is grace under pressure.
—**Ernest Hemingway**

The tool of a courageous heart can be gifted as we open up with intention to transform. The process begins with surrendering to life with eyes and heart open. This first step, as with most spiritual technologies, brings forth great fear because it requires letting go of existing coping mechanisms. This is like shedding our skin and being vulnerable to the elements. We are actually in the process of losing our personal self to find the inner peace and spiritually evolved gifts available only in the vortex of Self.

For many who dare to go beyond the existing boundaries of the finite self, with its limited positionalities, anything new can bring anxiety. Imagine the courage it takes to feel more you and less you and less fragmented and more whole. It is not one of the most automatic or easiest things to do, especially when challenged to label something or bring it from a past that only exists in memories. Keeping old concepts appears safe in the beginning and, at times, needed, but the problem with doing this old trick is that it halts our lessons and stops our growth. This happens because any choice from the past can create a consequence that now needs to be undone and will surely stall our spiritual growth.

In my life, whenever I tried to control the outcome, I received exactly what I alone created from an entrenched, often unconscious patterning. These solo endeavors out of alignment with Self usually left me unfulfilled. I found this particularly relevant in my relationships as I repeatedly felt the urge to seek revenge if and when attacked or felt a perceived slight. I was stuck creating outcomes that were fruitless. I did, however, eventually get unstuck by using several tools and was able to move into the newness of surrender. The courageous heart led the way as I practiced forgiveness with more understanding and humility as I acquired the skills needed to manage this angry, long-standing dark teacher.

Newness stands in the wisdom of your heart with unfathomable faith and a commitment to be fully in what is happening at that time. As seekers who are welcoming the courageous heart as a journeying partner, our goal is to say yes to all that occurs in our lives, to the best of our abilities. We can do this in any way that is comfortable. Prayer, church, self-help, yoga, meditation, and contemplation are only a few methods. Once we couple up with this powerful tool, our own unique soul expressions will emerge as Self expresses itself more in our daily lives. When we open the door to this helpful energy, we often have feet in both worlds. We open our eyes to the new and can allow ourselves to still evolve at our own pace while holding on to old choices that feel comfortable, even if they are fruitless. We get to decide what meets our needs by comparing outdated patterns as we build the courage to move into the newness that can help us evolve.

Evolution requires you to be other than you are in this moment—and other than you will be in the next. If we stay too safe in worn-out patterns, such as denial or self-castigating thoughts, we might become physically sick. I have seen many examples showing that even physical illnesses can grow a courageous heart, even though it is not an intended route. I have seen many people fight cancer and other serious illnesses with a courage I was blessed to behold.

Once we begin the spiritual path, it pulls us forward in an assortment of ways. That's where the courage is needed most. When we use spiritual tools, such as surrender, and become more tuned to our divine eyes and ears, our awareness of all divine options improves. The lessons on earth are not easy. Consider the lessons humility forces you to learn. There are occasions when you might feel you are not equal to those you need at times, due to your dependency on them. To remedy this, we must see others as divine placeholders. When we trust that we are not victims, contrast will cease to offer its sharp and tender conflicts.

The courageous heart allows us to move past rigidity. The human heart is always caught up in the lessons of duality, and it struggles with the unfamiliar. As our courage grows and we are led by the higher vibration of this enabler, we can move down the spiritual path, whether we are conscious or not. This version of the spiritual heart feels deeper in experience and has more ability to hold its truths. Everything on the spiritual journey is divinely placed and inspired. I realized that by being courageous, I could better thrive within any storm. You can be buffeted by the most vicious winds and the most violent repercussions and still see them meaningfully. This is the gift of the courageous heart. As the strength of this grace-filled tool embodies you and makes a cocoon around you, your job is to sharpen your ability to listen to your heart and the wisdom of its higher-vibration language.

As stated earlier, the law of duality plays a big part as a teacher on earth. As we awaken to this helpful but sometimes painful law, we see how we can know the best choices only in contrast to the worst. We call them *good* in contrast to what we call *bad*.

To move to the higher levels of heart, we must first balance and become aware of the human heart. The human heart is as vulnerable as a moth without wings. The courageous heart is as impenetrable as a warrior's shield. The human heart can die empty and defeated. The courageous heart can die blazing with light. The human heart can live without reason. The courageous heart can live with great purpose. This version of illuminated heart is love and light. The human heart is capable of hate and darkness. The human heart also contains divine gifts. It is the first doorway into the spiritual realms and to the experience of sacred love, usually through conditionality, pain, and attachments. The human heart is the home of duality. It is an important earth-plane experience. In the human heart, there is always the choice of love or hate, communion or separation, light or darkness. All choices hold the potential for growth. We choose. We walk. It takes great courage to do many things on earth, especially things that relate to the body or relationships. Once we have consciously taken on the vessel of the courageous heart, we can learn to face the most fragile situations. We can emerge as leaders of compassionate choice as our spiritual work allows us the opportunity to awaken.

The personal self can act like a stunt double by helping us prepare for the entrance of the Self. The courageous heart is an integration of the illuminated heart and the best parts of the human heart. The ability of the illuminated heart to hold the wisdom of unconditional love coupled with the courage to go beyond the limited dualistic tendencies of the human heart calls the Self with great fidelity. The courageous heart is a spiritual tool and mindset that brings on the illuminated heart. The illuminated heart, being a gift of grace, brings with it all that is sacred. This higher-vibration version of the human heart allows us to go beyond our previous limits and live with more of the illuminated unconditional love held on the soul level. The blending of all three hearts transcends limitation and gives life a vibrancy unparalleled by natural experience. The human heart coupled with the courageous heart then calls forth the illuminated heart, thus paving the way for Self. The illuminated heart does not have the tendency to give in to fear, as the human heart does, and it has the wisdom of Self to help us discern our choices. Living from this heart gives us more access to divine mind and the wisdom needed to live on earth with more joy and peace. The illuminated heart holds the love of all, of everything and of everyone. At this heart level, there is no dualism or split intention. There is only oneness. Love is unconditional. There are no exceptions. Having a true spiritual intention ignites the longing for this spiritual heart; this is the gift of being a spiritual being. The illuminated heart cherishes all it touches. There is nothing to forgive. There is nothing to explain. The courageous heart is one of the gateways that welcomes divine love to the earthly plane and can be the portal for illumination.

When we look at the basics of courage, we see that holding its mindset helps us face difficulty or danger with wisdom. It utilizes fear and initiates wise action, bravery, and valor. When we look at this vibration energy as a color, we see a vibrant red.

This is best illustrated as we notice a predominant color in the fashioning of businessmen's ties. Many refer to red as a power color. It holds us upright, present, and clear when we feel off-center and misaligned.

If we are using the courageous heart as a growth technology, there are many things to consider and many questions to ask. Most of us struggle with the others in our lives. Even though we allow courage to be present, we must still have self-love and use wisdom to live on earth. We should never let toxicity rule our lives. With the tools described in this book, we must clear a path through the debris of many storms. Even when our struggles have been jettisoned from our daily lives and thoughts and no longer flash through our minds and emotions, we must ask ourselves whether we have the courage to go into the black hole of the personal self to grow further. Can we let go of the victimhood that blocks growth? If we look deeply at courage, we see that it is linked with honesty. Can we ask the right questions? Perhaps only with courage. Please consider the following questions in summery of this chapter:

- Is there something I have chosen not to see in the past that I can see now?
- Whom can I speak to or rely on for support now?
- What resources are available to me to process my feelings?
- How is my fear leading me to my inner wisdom?

With courage, we can move through the limitations inherent in human experience and recognize that the real struggle is to evolve past self and fully be. We can then understand that the spiritual experience—when seen clearly—observes all human experience through the neutral witness with a courageous heart to inspire harmony and unconditional love. We take the spiritual journey mostly by surrendering our beliefs in inevitability (*Something bad will happen*) and separation (*Source is somewhere else*), which dominate the natural mind. We can then embrace faith as a new guide and direction. The light of the courageous heart can lead the way.

In summary, one can easily see through personal, local, and global experience that life in a realm that has duality and cause and effect as teachers is going to be challenging. Spiritual seekers eventually realize that coming to this realm is not a punishment, despite how it feels, and that divinity is all around us. The beauty of spiritual technologies and our persistence in using them gives us inner peace, which then resonates as a loving extension for the greater good. We must strive daily to see the divine interior being revealed in all that occurs. We must let our hearts guide us as often as possible. The human heart is the part of the natural mind that holds all valuable attachments dear and can easily turn up the volume of fear and doubt at any time. The courageous heart is helpful as it motivates this limited part of the natural mind to welcome all on the path of soul evolution.

> The Heart participates more strongly in what is happening in the depths of the soul as it is the link between body and soul more clearly than any other aspect of mind.
> —Edith Stein

PART 2

CHAPTER 14
COMPANION TOOLS

It does not matter how slowly you go, as long as you do not stop.
—**Confucius**

Please keep in mind the following questions as you proceed:

1. What are your spiritual goals?
2. How far have you gotten in reaching your spiritual goals?
3. What is working, and what is not working?
4. Are you stuck in any way?
5. What are your obstacles?
6. How willing are you to see through new eyes?
7. How confident or certain are you of your success in evolving into your Self?

The following companion mindsets and practices are designed to accentuate and enhance a seeker's practice of the previously observed instruments for personal and spiritual evolution. I once heard from an AA old-timer that Bill Wilson, the founder of Alcoholics Anonymous, constantly urged people who wished to remain sober to do "everything and all" to progress. I find this statement to be the best description of the amount of study, practice, and mental focus needed to evolve. This constructive use of our creative power drives us to transform our natural mind and personal self into the Self. A compassionate use of devotion is to practice thoughts and behaviors that help us to keep our commitments. The first practice ritual that corrected my vision was to keep a phrase in my mind that I believed was of a loving vibration. For example, I used "I am love" early and often to quell my loneliness until I could sustain the feeling of love more consistently. This single-pointed ritual was the harnessing of positive thought that helped me to see my world more through the lens of love, not fear. This desire sources from an essential core of divinity and is the workhorse for our victory over fear.

My parents had a tough marriage, and it was often hard to be in my house. When I could not sustain joy in my emotional and mental bodies, I found joy in sports. I devoted my time, effort, study, and financial resources to becoming a lacrosse player. Every day, I would care for my equipment and imagine shots and moves I would make on the field. I then would physically practice all aspects of the game for hours and project my success as a college player. I would wake up and immediately do strengthening drills. My desire at that time was for competence and respect, but as a consequence, I transformed my athletic abilities on a moment-to-moment basis. I would utilize humility and meekness as I watched films and observed peers try moves and perform in ways that were out of my preexisting beliefs about my capabilities.

My devotion still drives me to stretch my abilities and to think, act, and hope for betterment. When I use this tool to overcome my fears, I already have an existing template of desire of what transforming myself would take. I always have a book or an article in my car or at my workplace to read as I go through my day. I interject spirit-based concepts into my mind's chatter from the moment I awake until my final personal inventory at night. I plan actions and allocate time for ritual, meditation, and being in nature. I constantly use my mistakes and sojourns back into my fear-filled personal self to remind myself to persevere in the use of the tool needed. I attend spirit-based trainings, and I found a teacher who was right for my interest in finding peace through metaphysical study. I complete every assignment she gives, even if it creates dark feelings and forces me to look at my character defects. I realized early on in my own journey, and continue to realize as I help others, that being negative is easier. Devotion, coupled with meaningful desire, is effective in its ability to prevail over negativity.

Most seekers overlook the tendency we have to hold the status quo, and our lack of acknowledgment of this proclivity makes it common for us to overlook it in our self-examinations. Being awake to both our positive and our negative aspects requires effort and devotion. As I practice any tool, devotion comes in handy in helping to retrain my spiritual perspective to be the template through which I envision a new earth. The old world saw me struggle to love myself, which was a battle against my unworthiness and an existing toxic belief system. The new world is one of striving for automatic forgiveness and unconditional love.

This pointed intention to become devoted to our evolution is the foundation for using any of the following tools and for unveiling Self. This harbinger of divine essence exists only in the states of peace and joy. Along with devotion, I realized that to be honest, I had to be both rigorous and rigid in resolve. Using devotion with the transformational tool of honesty is a powerful way to progress in character and evolve in consciousness. Honesty is a prerequisite for all spiritual and psychological success. This tool helps us to attach to truth and use it to uncover the fear-based belief systems that keep us shackled to the past and to its pain. Honesty can also bring divine order to positive social interactions that are built on trust. As I learned more about spiritual advancement, I realized that the wholeness I aspired to had no room for dishonesty in any form. I had to be willing to look at my thoughts, motives, and behaviors with an eye of rigorous honesty and promptly admit any less-than-honest words or actions. I soon realized I used dishonesty to protect my natural mind from either rejection or persecution through self-deception. The tool of externalization proved again to be of great relief at that time. I then learned to use a journaling device called the wasteland, which allowed me to write down the personal self's motive behind my deception and to explore without shame why I needed to use a dishonest mechanism to meet a need. The dishonest mechanisms were a wasteland of my worst intentions and most self-centered choices. Externalizing my destructive belief system helped me to release self-judgment and objectify traits that blurred my spiritual vision. I eventually found that all my dishonesty was my natural mind's way of protecting me from perceived attack, either external in the form of criticism or rejection or internal in the form of shame and guilt. The tool of rigorous honesty helped me to take inventory of my interactions and see when I was reacting out of fear. By first watching any dysfunctional system, I could write about it in journals, pray out loud, or speak about it with a friend or counselor in an attempt to uproot the dishonest system. I also had to learn to forgive myself as I probed into my moral inventory. I looked at parts of my character that originally had been denied but now could be used as raw material to see the direction needed to travel. This again reminded me to make use of the concept "All I am not is all I will be."

The real key to using this tool of honesty is to share and express our thoughts, actions, or intentions to both an internal inventory taker and an external source. As we become more adept with humility, our internal inventory taker can become more reliable. However, I found that I gained more clarity and had a better chance for honesty mostly through externalization. The hesitancy to externalize is triggered by the personal self's tendency to deny dishonest systems in an attempt to keep them in place to protect from shame and guilt. To paraphrase Socrates, all we do is for our perceived good. This tendency of the natural mind to hold on to manipulative and dishonest tendencies is its projection of the inevitable negative consequences mistakes can create.

I found the following practices helpful, as they allowed for clarity and release. I would tell on myself, stopping in the middle of a lie or an exaggeration to admit, "I'm sorry; that's wrong." People would be in awe of the admission and listen to what followed with renewed interest. When I used my journal to discuss my past mistakes or lack of integrity, it served as a confessional in which I could release the guilt and heal the shame. To use rigorous honesty, we must be devoted to watching the natural mind's tendency to put a spin on both past and present experiences. This satisfies the personal self's constant need for self-value through appearing special and thus reinforcing pseudo-self-esteem. Once I felt more spiritually whole, I no longer needed to be dishonest in an attempt to be special. I was then able to accept myself—not despite my character defects but because of them. This allowed me to teach others the same tool and, thus, to extend creation energy. That felt better than the disharmony of dishonesty. Rigorous honesty can become a state of being and, when practiced with compassion, is a healing model to others. All truth resonates and leads to a deeper safety in relationships and peace within mind.

The use of humility has been the most dynamic in my awakening. The amount of shame and guilt programmed into my natural mind at the beginning of my journey kept me from feeling peace without external distraction. The tool of humility was salvation from the natural mind's perception of victimhood and subsequent need to attack. I would punish either myself or others for perceived shortcomings, mistakes from the past, injustices, or anything that went against the insane measurement system of what was wanted. I practiced humility because it is the complete opposite of the natural mind's need to hide shortcomings, foster negative selfassessment, and thus block spiritual progress.

The term *radical* fits well with this tool because it can depict something that is completely different and goes in an opposite direction with conviction. My natural mind, in an attempt to perceive the personal self as valuable, is constantly on alert for vulnerability. In some cases, people would rather die than admit defeat or ignorance. Radical humility is the honest ownership of all our base human qualities and the acceptance of the need for sane technology and grace for clarity. Humility is the action of allowance and acceptance of the fact that the perception does not allow us to have all the answers and is prone to making assumptions. By using radical humility as a daily tool along with devotion and rigorous honesty, we transform our base human elements into compassion for others. Shame can then be transformed back into a loving reminder to be better, and guilt recedes to be felt as a decent regret for behavior that was attempted with the best intention capable at that time. By loosening up the attack on ourselves, we also allow others their humanness and are less judgmental and critical in general. In the words of Dr. David Hawkins, "Because of the ego's tendency towards ignorance most people are unable to be different, and thus are being run by endless programs and belief systems."

The reason for our defensiveness is our mind's tendency to own any negative habits or behavioral patterns because of guilt and shame. These two natural-mind default mechanisms are helpful only when used in certain situations; when they become states of being, we cannot access Self. But once we understand ourselves through the practice of humility, we can understand our dark character traits and no longer have to repress them.

I began to write down my most hated aspects, such as meanness, self-centered actions, and fears, in my journal. I also started telling people about my frailties and mistakes while teaching. These actions allowed me to lessen the shame by being received and supported with either laughter or validation when I discussed the issues in public. It appeared to me that I was speaking to and healing everyone who had the same expressed rancorous quality or who had made those mistakes. In ensuing public appearances, people would actively search me out after the class to express gratitude and care. People thanked me for having a life that worked well despite my obstacles. I spoke constantly about my making many decisions from a place of fearful unknowing and a lack of self-confidence. I also suffered from a loneliness that plagued me day and night. From these experiences, it appeared that my victory over shame was my greatest gift to others. I used humble thoughts, such as *If I could have done better, I would have*, *My pain helps me to connect to the pain of others and grows compassion*, *Just have a decent regret*, and *If I were perfect, I wouldn't be here*. These mantras allowed me to soften my judgmental self-talk and take responsibility for the pain caused either to myself or to others. I began to feel lovingly toward the qualities I had originally punished myself for, and I subsequently became more loving toward others. I could not judge another once I stood naked in my own natural mind's circus of insane systems. I was more compassionate and forgiving as I interacted with family, friends, and clients.

 I also developed a more devoted attitude that worked to transform my qualities into their polar opposites. I switched my anger into forgiveness, my dishonesty into honesty, and my fear into faith. Humility allowed me to see the natural healing inherent in the dualistic process of having a natural mind. My new neutral witness perspective attached to the belief that my essential goodness and love were already a potential in my spiritual nature, which then increased my confidence and helped to speed the process of my spiritual growth in general. Prior to this acceptance, I had seen salvation outside myself and felt powerless to acquire the qualities I needed to be a good dad or healer. By acceptance of my acrimonious personal tendencies, I could see them with more clarity before I acted on them. I could feel hidden tendencies rising up to be healed, because they weren't camouflaged by the states of shame and guilt. This made doing the opposite more automatic, until the new behavior or thought was involuntary. The use of rigorous honesty and single-minded devotion helped to allow humility to be effective due to the courage and introspection needed to do it daily. The natural mind is never going to rest until it becomes our author again, so these tools must be ever present and dynamic in our daily lives to beckon the wisdom of divine mind found within Self. Radical humility also serves to bring couples to a deepening level of intimacy as they reveal aspects of themselves that crave acceptance and healing. Relationships draw out the aspects of our splintered selves that are in need of love and healing. Radical humility heals to the extent that each person can be less guarded as he or she looks at him- or herself without blame. Then two people can move closer to the ultimate peace and safety of unconditionality in a relationship. I love myself and my wife, not in spite of our darkness but because it is a reflection of our potential as spiritual and emotional beings.

Once we are adept at using these wonderful technologies and their enabling cohorts, we can be introduced to one of the most powerful helpers of all: compassion. Once we become aware of the beauty and joy inherent in feeling unconditionally loved as a being, we can then see how the state of compassion naturally warms us and extends itself to others. The warmth of love is like the sun's rays extending their creative powers to life in all forms. Compassion is the form unconditional love takes in relationships as a practical unifying bond. The beauty of humility sets the stage for us to extend understanding and mercy as we journey in our personal self's struggle in imperfection, and we can then choose to extend humility in communion with other beings. Compassion works as a cleansing agent to the personal self's need for specialness and separation. Our earth apparatus, the natural mind, craves value but is often not interested in extending it. Unconditional love connects us to our true value, which then extends itself naturally through us out into the world.

I would practice being compassionate and of service to others by allowing them to make mistakes, fail, and act destructively without judgment. It eventually became more automatic to extend compassion to my clients and friends, but I would still attack myself with self-talk, such as "I should have known better." The bonding aspects of compassion come from the understanding that within me is the full potential to act destructively or divinely. I realized that within me is a connection to a collective smorgasbord of options that my personal self uses to accomplish its pleasure-seeking mission. I cannot judge others if I know they are also connected to these options. Through honesty and humility, I am aware of how limited I am because of these preexisting connections. A blessing of our focus on unconditional love is the emergence of humble feeling and perspective that the emergence of Self, while in a realm using time for clarity, is a work in progress. We are all of the same value on a spiritual level and are all deserving of understanding. Compassion reminds us that we are part of a whole family of evolving beings and inextricably part of one love. Once I extended compassion, I became better able to see love in others and practice forgiveness.

All spiritual technology helps to solidify compassion as a component of our own original spiritually loving state of being, thus making it a cornerstone in the development of a spiritual character. Compassion is the active part of the state of unconditional love. This love has as its innate nature a natural resonance that effects healing and harmonizes all in its radius.

Recently, I was eating lunch in a restaurant, when I became acutely aware of a little child being yelled at to behave. The father was frustrated with her misbehavior, and the child felt fear of the father's physical attack in the form of little hits on her legs. I applied compassion as a tool and instantly felt the fear of the child. I was tempted to overidentify with the child, but by utilizing humility, I remembered there are times when I also have the same tendency as the father to be impatient and to allow fear and public embarrassment to dictate my actions. I then extended love through silent prayer and found my judgment leaving, replaced with love for the little child in myself and compassion for the family of evolving beings. A short time later, she was on his lap and laughing.

Compassion can best be used by extension to self and others, starting with intention not to judge. I have become better in recent years at picking the most compassionate style of intervention and, with positive intention, understanding, and discernment, awaiting the prompt to act. I can be silent and hold the space, or I can ask if the person or people I'm uniting with need help in any way. I have found that when people give you permission to extend compassion, they receive its healing energy more fully. They also feel more empowered and will let the healing touch stay longer in their energy. I came to realize that when I forced compassionate actions or words, people often felt shame, and this created a blockage for compassion's reception. I often use this tool verbally in the form of self-disclosure to help validate others' fear and hurts. I use my own self-compassion as a guide to become more deeply invested in looking for the style of intervention my heart deems best for others. We can become acutely aware of what to extend to others if we take an in-depth inventory of what feels good for us. Using our personal self as a guide to help others is one of the most compassionate forms of healing both others and self. I use my wisdom and experience as a guide to extend help or just to extend compassionate intention. I can pray for the person or situation as I act in a way that keeps the dignity of the recipient foremost. The action can be either physical or material. It can be silent or verbal, but either way, warmth is being extended perfectly.

An aspect of compassion that is hard for some of us at first is the need to let others suffer while we stand by and don't intervene. We can always send the light of compassion through the loving energy of thought as we unify with another by recalling mutual experiences found in suffering. We are well served when we remember the lessons born out of suffering, and when held in gratitude, we are more likely to compassionately allow others to feel their dark lessons. Some of my greatest victories have come out of suffering. If we always took people out of suffering, we would not be practicing compassion, because we would be enforcing our agendas. I have come to see that the pain and the repression of the memory of suffering in ourselves can create a dispassionate agenda. We often need to work through our own struggles to feel victorious. These uncomfortable times feel like painful experiences but can be helpful in creating a spiritual character whose essential qualities give us more resiliency and courage. Anything that is not seen in the eyes of gratitude has not been seen in its truth, including experiences that first appear painful. All things are a call to prayer and serve to advance our experience of Self.

To experience the magic of the helper called meekness means to allow new information about our limitations or strengths to enter as a sharp or tender instructor. This helper is both an attitude and a quality of thought that comes from the belief that if we open our minds, we will receive guidance that is far better for us than anything our memory or experience held in the natural mind could communicate to us. This guidance can appear in magical ways or through mundane events, people, and circumstances. As I began to trust in my Self and ask for guidance directly through revelation or vivid dreaming, I was shown magical things. These healing dreams are filled with symbols that often create feelings of awe and stimulate revelatory moments once deciphered. As I evolved, it became more evident to me that I hadn't integrated much about anything spiritual into my daily behavior. I had read much and attended many psychological seminars and schools but still seemed devoid of self-love. I was still people-pleasing and seemed to feel lack and longing in all areas of my life. As I look back, I see that I even taught the concept of meekness without actually being meek. I was actually teaching what I wished to learn. I saw that I hadn't integrated spiritual technology enough, and as a result, I consistently couldn't avoid regressive trips back to the use of my limited personal tools to cope with difficult problems.

The following story illustrates this point well. My son Christian was testing my patience by bouncing a ball in the room while I was writing this book. I extended first compassion and then forgiveness for a short time, until I screamed at him to stop. He then triggered my guilt with his dejected look, and I was left feeling the limits of my fragile patience. Once my practice of patented patience ended, I reverted back to the manipulative devices of power and size.

I soon realized the practice of meekness is more helpful when used in tandem with one or all of the companion tools. I found that through humility and honesty, I was much more willing to work through any lesson. I saw that one had to work hard to stay open to the fact that becoming spiritual was a change in character and thought programming, not an academic pursuit, and presented many challenges. I had to digest these tools, and once they were properly digested, I had the option to act from the tool instead of my fear. The tool of meekness helped me to viscerally learn that being something is different from knowing something. Meekness opens the door to integration, and through practice and devotion, transformation can occur. I began to see that I needed to learn on a deeper level. I was learning in order to appear smart and speak well to others. At that time, I read about how Moses had been able to change the course of history by practicing meekness. To me, it appeared Moses was a happy learner and was able to be changed and guided in a way that set the pace for us all. To be happy learners, we must be willing to await guidance and to surrender our will to the ever-present spiritual teacher in Self. When I began to practice meekness, I would maintain a daily openness while I awaited new information. Spiritual truths always feel new, even if the package by which they appear has familiar wrapping. For instance, an old song or reading can feel new, and a significance once overlooked can emerge. This transformation tool was so powerful that I began to listen more to my intuition while in prayer and through contemplation. Meekness allowed me a feeling of freedom as if I had sprouted wings and learned how to fly. Being mighty in my openness, I stayed the course during difficult learning periods when I wanted to negate lessons or move on.

To practice meekness, we must first believe we don't have total clarity in ourselves. This allows us to turn our willingness to a source of experience and information outside our natural minds. Once I had faith that this veiled source was there, it soon began appearing in books, movies, and all the lessons of daily interactions with my neighbors. I would get up every morning and put on my meekness cloak to walk through my day. Whenever I realized I was blocking information or discounting it, I stopped to contemplate those lessons particularly. I kept my mind open and allowed wisdom to be introduced into my insight digestive system, first through thought and then through feeling, which led to practice and transformation. If I was not ready for the lesson, it seemed it was stored in my divine mind to await a future trigger. I especially watched young children at play and people with physical disabilities to become aware of innocence and purity, and I began to see the divine thread of instructional goodness in all people, events, and circumstances.

I interpreted the Bible phrase "to inherit the earth" to mean I could create a human existence based on spiritual truth, not my natural mind's self-centered needs or insecurities. I could have my feet on the strong foundation of meekness as I dared to be different every day and even dared to be what I didn't believe possible. Meekness helped me to acknowledge others' intelligence without feeling jealousy, as I now saw in them specialized teachings designed for my evolution by a loving higher teacher. No matter who or what was teaching, I was always learning from the divine teacher within. I went through my day with my happy learner glasses firmly in place.

During one period in my life, I had a supervisor who was critical and condescending. I originally saw her as an enemy and myself as her misunderstood victim, which stopped any learning I could have obtained about myself. It stalled my learning so much that it hindered my evolution as a therapist and a spiritual person. When I heard about meekness, I began working to stop my judgment of her and her feedback, which allowed me to see that she thought I didn't tell her my truth to keep peace with staff and patients. I realized her criticisms were usually directed at the manipulative behavior my fear-based personal self used to stave off rejection. It then became clear I was discounting my own natural anger and allowing others, including her, too much authorship of my life. Only when I used the mighty tool of meekness did I get this powerful, lifechanging revelation. The rest of my supervisor's and my relationship was still cold, but I had moved on in my own consciousness.

I also learned from the tool of meekness how I allowed others to judge me as unworthy. This came from my existing template of shame and guilt that I carried from childhood, which I reverted to in challenging times. The practical entrance to using meekness is to keep the phrase "What's the lesson?" in my mind constantly. I also would write the lesson in my journal to allow it to unfold in clarity as I observed how my natural mind was invested in keeping me shamed and stuck in an attempt to minimize future pain. The tool of meekness is a constant state now, even when my feelings tell me I think I know something. I use meekness to automatically surrender any useless bit of knowledge for the better version yet to come. To be happy learners is to give ourselves the greatest gift—meekness—which we can then extend as a gift to others. Once we model meekness as a daily occurrence, people notice our changes, and some inquire about it, asking, "Did you lose weight?" or "Did you go on vacation recently?" or saying, "You seem more tolerant." These statements are others' intuitive readings of your freedom from the natural mind's need to be right. Now people, even my patients and adversaries, can be my teachers. In dark suits or light, all teachers are sent from the same loving source.

> I am not bound to win, but I am bound to be true.
> I am not bound to succeed, but I am
> bound to live up to what I have.
> —Abraham Lincoln

CHAPTER 15
ATTITUDINAL GRATITUDE

If the only prayer you ever say in your entire life is thank you, it will be enough.
—**Meister Eckhart**

Parents who are intent on loving begin their children's spiritual and social development by reminding them to say thank you often. Children learn this by mimicking, modeling, and repetition. My kids get wonderful material things and an abundance of loving attention regularly and, hence, see gifts and affection as commonplace. Many of us, whether we had sparse childhoods or abundant childhoods, tend to try hard to give our children what they need and want out of love or guilt. However, if we are not careful, occasions of receiving cherished items and loving attention can lose the lesson of gratitude.

I practice teaching my kids to enjoy what they already have and to give thanks for what cannot be bought. When gratitude is used strictly by the natural mind, our personality can appear socially grateful but lacks authenticity. At these times, I have used gratitude to get what I wanted and present myself as gracious in order to manipulate or protect from being judged or emotionally wounded. I would appear thankful to buy others' favor and set up situations to continue to receive. This practice came from the constant feeling of lack and fear that I wouldn't get what I needed from an unsafe world. While I expressed gratitude, it was gratitude used in fear, not based on good intention.

One specific incident in college taught me the proper use of gratitude. I had to start junior year at college in an apartment off campus because of poor grades due to my paying attention only to socializing and lacrosse. My parents brought furniture from home when they drove up to fix my apartment as I tried to begin again. We were not rich, and my tuition was already stretching them financially. My poor grades made them afraid for my future, and they were taking one final chance on that year. I worked with them to set up my apartment, and as I sat resting, I noticed my mom bent over with back pain and worry as she carried up more stuff from the car. I finally saw her as lovingly sacrificing her health and money to give me another chance. I got a flash of gratitude for the opportunity to go to college and to have such love available. My grades never went below an A in all the school I attended thereafter. I must note now that forty years later, as I recount this story on these pages, I am crying tears of gratitude for my mom.

Appreciation and Self-love are the most important aspects we could ever nurture. Appreciation of others and even the personal self is the closest vibrational match to source energy we can experience on earth. I learned to eventually use the beauty of gratitude as a lens to see the world from the vantage point of grace. Gratitude calls in what is wished for and opens the door for the delivery of all that is intended using the law of attraction, an immutable law that guarantees if we combine desire with gratitude and complete faith, we have to receive our wishes. As gratitude became more automatic in my conscious mind, my ability to manifest my desires became more efficient and immediate.

My spiritual vision helps me to see that all unfolds as a gift for our evolution. My natural mind constantly needs to be reminded of this because of its inability to stay constant in the positive belief that I am truly living in a state of worthiness. It lives mostly in lack, ingratitude, and a longing for more. Gratitude allows for peace because it instantly fills our voids with faith in attraction of what is needed in real time. Gratitude also acts as an antidote to the natural mind's default of the need to play victim. I began to experience its beauty myself as a powerful creator once I harnessed the law of attraction more efficiently. Seeing through the lens of gratitude with its escort, humility, also kept me from making harmful choices that my victimization persona would have justified. I had to try my hardest to practice using gratitude when I was in the presence of the suffering inherent in dark journeys, such as depression, illness, and tragedy. These experiences can be helpful teachers in our becoming gratitude incarnate. This new vision-correction tool helps all around by extending our understanding that life's occurrences are a perfect gift in our evolution. The tool of gratitude also serves to hold up a mirror to our neighbors to reflect what they give and do with love. People feel closer to us when we are genuinely grateful for interactions.

I was able to better feel the tool of gratitude by doing a physical meditation. This simple ritual is done in two movements accompanied by three words. I would stand erect with my torso twisted to the right and my hands in a receiving posture as if to grab a tray from behind me. I then would say out loud or silently, "Thank you." Then I would turn to the front and motion as if handing off the tray with the word *here*. This meditation mimics the exact nature of creation energy as it passes through us on the way to extension.

I began to see that we are all conduits of love energy. The fewer fear blockages we have, the more love flows. Gratitude eventually becomes a fixed attitude or set of beliefs that create a perspective by which to look at all life. This attitude can be triggered by a thank-you or by connecting to a fixed point in nature, such as a sunrise or a snow-covered mountain. Nature shows us grace constantly in its awesome power and beauty. I also realized that a wonderful reminder of grace was my body. This communication device and earth suit is a miracle. My wife is training to be a nurse and constantly teaches us how amazing our bodies are. I also use my breath to express gratitude in meditation as I mindfully repeat, "Thank you," saying the word *thank* on the inhalation and *you* on the exhalation. This brings back my attitude and pushes my fear and lack away.

Gratitude is an especially powerful centering mechanism when we feel we are in a dark place or need a spiritual boost after a trying temptation or challenge. I especially like when I can see gratitude in my own work as a cocreator. I am now able to sit back and see a good class or a compassionate interaction as an extension of love. I can even stand in awe of the power of love emerging in the emergence and presence of Self. I am also closer to understanding other tools, such as humility and kindness, because of gratitude's ability to move me outside my personal-self-centered world. When I move outside myself and into meekness, forgiveness greets me at the door and leads me to the beauty of compassion, which actively transforms the world. When we look around in wonder through gratitude, it also makes what is excellent in others belong to us.

As gratitude is a way of being kind and appreciative to an outside source, kindness is a way of being in the world that honors the innate divinity in all things. I began to practice kindness as a specific mindset by seeing acts of kindness in daily occasions. These acts served as a warm-up to practice bigger acts of compassion, until I eventually saw that each act, big or small, was of the same value and had equal effect. To spiritually aware people, small is big, and what you do inside will be projected outside. In perception, we see what we look for. I started talking kindly to myself when I made a mistake, whereas before, I would obsess with guilt and shame. This simple, loving voice of kindness would say, for example, "I did the best I could," "Just take the lesson, and then move on and give it away," and "My humanness connects me to others through compassion." These rote and memorized dialogues were simple and acted like a loving mother's voice or a papa's right counsel in times when I would have suffered in the illusion of needed punishment. It became apparent that I would be better served to start incorporating kindness into my internal dialogue. Once I realized I was resonating with a critical energy originating from my shame and guilt, I quickly set out through the use of this tool to change that thought stream into one of kindness. I like simple lessons and thoughts because of my analytical nature and overactive natural mind's critic; hence, I use this tool as a constant companion in my day.

Using kind acts in a social situation always helps to relieve the possibility of escalating emotions. Simple acts, such as holding a door, without the agenda of being recognized give my neighbors a message that love is present in their world. If the recipient does not recognize the act, then at least it serves as a positive reflection of a loving potential inherent in the personal self. I am acting kind to myself when I change from a needy, self-centered view of life and move closer to bringing on Self as a full-time companion. Any victory over this tendency is a tremendous kindness to my spiritual character as it emerges with certainty and confidence. The practice of no harm through simple kindness extends both ways and begins each endeavor as a positive possibility.

I have used kindness most powerfully when dealing with hurtful teachers in my life, such as a critical boss or a mean neighbor. I often use a simple thank-you to neutralize the conflict that can emerge from my sensitivity once I've been hurt or criticized. The action of kindness can give me breath and create a neutral space in which I surrender to the lesson of the moment instead of impulsively choosing harmfully. Using this wonderful tool also gives each moment a new sacred meaning. I can use each occasion externally or internally as if I asked for an opportunity to practice kindness. Kindness is best used behind the scenes, as with a good deed no one sees or a chore finished without fanfare. As my teacher explained, when we act with the need to be appreciated, it negates the spiritual benefit of the action. I practiced this recently when our kitchen was filled with dirty dishes and a full dishwasher. I cleared the washer and filled it with the sink's deposit of dishes. Now, you might say this is my job anyway, but my wife had gone to bed and told me not to do it, because she was going to do it in the morning. I would usually either complain about the situation or wash the dishes with much need for praise. I acted kind to myself because I furthered my humble practice and made the work a prayer. I acted kind to my family because they got up to a clean kitchen.

There is also a type of kindness I like to use called sweetness. Sweetness is an act that has the specific ability to make the other person feel unique and special. When people say, "That's sweet," they are usually responding to a feeling of being seen and appreciated as a special being. A card or a kind gift can have a major healing impact on others, and because of the unique ability love has to touch all involved, it has a healing impact on us in the giving. I suggest that you be creative and use your imagination with all these tools, but you will especially like how the use of kindness resonates. I use my kindness-coat morning ritual as a way to bring this tool to conscious attention. I use the simple act of putting on a shirt to remember to arm myself with kindness. Kindness can also be used instead of a more direct and overt act of compassion or love. These energies are often too powerful for some people to receive. It also appears that people are uncomfortable with love, so the use of kindness is easier to accept. People have belief systems that limit or deflect love and compassion due to love's previous discomfort or perceived obligatory nature. Simple kindness is just simple love and goes over well in situations when love, not reward, is our only agenda.

My first job as a social worker was at a drug treatment center for teens. As I looked around the therapy rooms, I noticed slogans designed to change dysfunctional mental concepts. The slogan that stood out first and foremost was "To be aware is to be alive." I didn't realize that this implied self-awareness as well as a reminder to be vigilant while walking in a world of danger and temptation. I was unaware at the time that my inability to sustain peace and joy was a result of toxic thoughts, not necessarily a bad childhood. This gave birth to my relationship with the cohort tool of vital vigilance, which soon became the active mechanism that trained me to develop a watcher in my own head.

When under stress, I would do guided visualizations, putting myself in a nature scene, to gain peace. As I sat in traffic imagining a favorite beach, I suddenly realized that someone in my daydream was watching me sit on that lifeguard stand. I was then aware of myself as an observing consciousness. I was watching myself on a mind screen. My mind had a watcher who could monitor my natural mind's dialogue like a person watching a movie. At the time, I was still unsure what was watching me sit on that beach, but after much more reading and contemplation, I realized it was the divine mind of Self. I then set out with intention through vigilance to build a familiarity with this overlord of spiritual truth in any way possible. This self-observant thought exercise involved imagining a pair of new glasses. These vision changers prompted me to focus the watcher in three ways: what I said, why I said it, and what I expected from saying it. I was now analyzing the *why* in all things mindfully, not the *what* I said.

This divine filtering system triggered by the use of vigilance still gives me the best chance to communicate lovingly in wisdom. The natural mind usually communicates with the personal self and others with an agenda of being noticed or manipulating something in some way in its quest for attention to help further define its boundaries as an individual, separate entity. We must remember that this is its limited mission and is perfect to ignite a great desire to unfold the Self. Vital vigilance brings with it the best chance that our interactions are truly about giving unidirectionally. This is always the domain of higher consciousness through an unconditional love that keeps us in the flow of creation-energy extension. Giving in this advanced style simply means that by extending anything outside ourselves, we are also the recipient. We can accomplish this only if we do so without the hope or condition of reward.

By using vigilance as an intentional natural-mind watchdog, I soon realized I could have a delay system in my head for words said, choices made, and movements attempted. I began to transfer focus to the neutral witness and soon was able to make choices with less impulsive energy and more compassion. I discovered I could choose from what felt more like my spiritual heart. It also became clear that focusing on why words were thought or said was a great way to know the personal limitations that created pain. This drastically changed my friendships and marriage because I made fewer hurtful, arrogant, and self-serving comments. I could then monitor streams of attitudes and beliefs about topics, people, and events and let go of opinions and conclusions that turned out to be naive assumptions based on insecurity and limited information. I became my own loving parent and then, through vigilance and focus, replaced outdated belief systems, such as *Everyone has to like me* and *I have to help everybody*. I eventually realized that I was the only one who had to like me and that people had to suffer their own choices in order to grow. This helpful change saw a more objective watcher on duty with vigilant scrutiny.

To have vigilance is to be alert to our intentions. The law of attraction states that our intentions, even subconscious ones, create the circumstances of our lives. My intentions had been attracting negativity into my life at times. The ability to be aware helped me attract circumstances, actions, and others with more clarity. I judged these things only against the template of effective or ineffective, helpful of hurtful, loving or unloving, harmless or harmful. I also realized I couldn't control what came into the natural mind but only what I held in mind. This revelation in particular freed me from relentless negative self-judgments once I was convinced I wasn't the author of some of the more heinous and dysfunctional dialogues my natural mind entertained. I eventually became a student of new ways to feel and teach a loving attitude toward the whole process of my limited and potentially harmful personal self. I learned not to identify my self-value by the stream of thoughts in my natural mind's dialogue and, through awareness, became better at looking at my life through my divine mind as a means to feel my worth. Knowing that love is a state of being, not an emotion that can be decreased or increased in any way, is heaven on earth.

Vital vigilance is a powerful, transformative tool that also allows us to see others' behaviors and lives as examples of effective intention or hurtful choices not to be taken personally. I learned a lot through being vigilant to others' successes or mistakes. I didn't have to reinvent the wheel; I watched others interact in their worlds by using the tools they had available at the time. I eventually stopped judging them as people and became a student of their choices. This was facilitated by the mindset of unconditionality. I even grew to see the commonality of all experience as opportunities for growth through compassion.

I came to see that familiar things in our environment most often trigger our use of any tool and that illness can also play a major role in our learning of many lessons. The body is probably the most common trigger. Illness most often slows us down and puts us in a better position to take personal inventory so that with vigilance, learning can be accelerated and digested at a better pace. Vigilance is much more effective if we focus through neutrality. I often move my conscious awareness to my heart, which is where I believe my watcher resides in my body. Then I ask questions. Sometimes I ask while placing my hands on my heart and feel for my answers as they emerge in vibrations, feelings, and, ultimately, words. I also use my journal to put my opinions on paper to bolster my ability to discern between heart and head. According to *A Course in Miracles*, the natural mind wants to use its beauty in its delusional system, unless it is brought under vigilant scrutiny by the light of love.

Once we see our lives and our world with more clarity, we will need more specific vision-corrective devices to navigate the conflict-ridden journey into Self. The escort called total tolerance is a tool that can get the dirty job done. Tolerance not only is helpful in dealing with the variant levels of maturity and consciousness of the sacred others we live with but also is a great help in allowing us to grow and regress in our normal style. As time went on, I realized I had expected life to follow random self-pleasuring templates that were for the most part unconsciously built. I wanted traffic to be a certain way; I wanted people to do what I wanted when I wanted; and most importantly, I needed people to treat me a certain way for me to feel loved. I came to the tool of tolerance as a necessity to exist in a world with many demands. I was protecting my shame-filled personal self from feeling out of control in a world I deemed unsafe. I soon realized that whenever I was angry or frustrated, my feeling was not because of what had happened but because of what hadn't happened. The realization of this natural tendency was helpful to gain more peace and joy. The construct of my natural thought process was basically designed to meet my own needs, and when my needs were fulfilled, I felt pleasure as a reward. Through vigilance, I became aware of the fact that I had arbitrary templates of expectations placed on others, their behaviors, and, ultimately, the external world in general. This created a constant unreal standard by which I judged all things according to these conditions. Total tolerance began my attempt to allow life to be on life's terms, not my often unconscious terms. I used my vigilance and neutral witness to look at my existing templates and eventually adjusted them to be more loving, peaceful, and tolerant.

The use of tolerance was especially helpful when applied to my many failed efforts to stay in the vortex of Self. This was especially true when I was tired and stressed or felt unloved and lonely. I tolerated the dark teachers and used as many tools as I could remember to get through those trying periods. I also used total tolerance as a new template, even in mundane situations, such as a long line at the supermarket or someone driving badly in my vicinity. I still had fear-driven feelings of anger, frustration, and intolerance and often had to take a long breath, triggering my use of the breath ritual four-seven-eight, which I did three times in a row, breathing in for a four count, holding the breath for a seven count, and releasing the breath to an eight count. This floods the brain with oxygen and reduces intolerance through the body. I also used mental slogans, such as "It's all good" or "Let go, and let God," to better tolerate situations I perceived as out of control. I also had to use tolerance as a form of internal self-talk due to feelings of shame and guilt.

One of the biggest challenges in the learning of tolerance can be our tendency to play a victim. The victim-and-victimizer default is the body-mind's biggest defense mechanism. I needed to allow myself to be human and to tolerate the mistakes made by myself and others. The dialogue of tolerance allows for the understanding of attack and its forgiveness. Its vibration consists of a loving voice speaking reassuring and positive words. When appropriate, I also use humor to recontextualize a problem or mistake. Tolerance is an open door for more enjoyment through release of control. The use of total tolerance also allows me to let people act in ways they need to act. This tool, when coupled with forgiveness, minimizes my relationship problems. I can then use unconditional love and compassion once I begin to tolerate. The more I tolerate my own humanness through humility, the more I am able to extend this tolerance to others. This brings my internal peace and joy to my outside world in the form of attracting more positive people and more positive responses. The real payoff in using this tool is the freedom it brings to each occasion. I see more beauty and learn valuable lessons from these occurrences now that I am not using my energy to fit the new situation into my existing fear-based construct. I can see more love in the world and have fewer occasions of guilt because I act better and am less likely to negatively judge my neighbors.

I grew up in an unsafe world as a child and developed a fearful template that spurred me on constantly. The short-lived triumphs from my fear-based template didn't give me the peace that total tolerance does. Tolerance also helps me to accept, not resist, life lessons, which then work to minimize my need to repeat the lessons. For example, by using tolerance with a neighbor who obviously didn't want to be friendly, I minimized attempts to befriend him and make him like me. This gave him the space he needed to grow in trust, and eventually, we became friends. My original programming said that he had to be nicer, and if not, I would judge him or make him like me through people-pleasing. Instead, I was able to tolerate my own human need to be liked without judgment and thus allow him his choice not to like me. Through humility and meekness, I also realized that I am extremely friendly and overwhelming to some types of people, so through compassion, I was able to tolerate his perceived unfriendliness without retaliation in the form of confrontation or contemptuous judgment.

Total tolerance is also powerful in that it allows us not to react fearfully to protect ourselves but instead to remain nonjudgmental and have a chance to make a better choice. Previously, when my expectations weren't matched, I resisted and fought to change things, often with conflict and heavy-handed control. I am now learning through these tools that

I no longer have to be in conflict or control and am able to use more creative ways to change myself. The true power of changing my mindset to divine mind is the formula to change external situations. It is becoming clearer as I journey with devotion that my only real human and spiritual need is to stand in the vortex of Self as much as possible. The spiritual vision by which I now see reveals a world that unfolds perfectly for the evolution of all involved. Tolerance is a gateway to continue to progress to higher states of surrender. I get joy even from previously intolerable people, situations, and experiences. The practical use of slogans and mental images to see life through an attitude of gratitude helps immediately when life throws a curveball our way.

As a complement to all previously mentioned helpers, the tool of stellar stillness is a welcomed gift. Although it would appear that stillness is quiet and unassuming, its ability to be an abiding presence and act in subtle and pervasive ways can light a path for tremendous clarity. When I use stellar stillness, I experience the peace of spiritual practice in the moment and immediately am transported into an eternal now that allows for all tools to be more effective. Many religious scriptures and self-help books give ultimate credit to this tool as a predominant expression of divine presence. I have found that in stillness, I can learn better and react with more logic and clarity of purpose.

For example, I once used stillness while having lunch with my wife on vacation. She said something I judged, and I rolled my eyes. I saw her notice my passive-aggressive action, and I quickly said I was sorry and became still as she explained herself (ridiculed and berated me). I remained still and attentive as she let go of her anger. I held the space in stellar style, and the potential conflict faded, so we could spend the rest of lunch in quasi-peace.

Many times in my life, I have been at major crossroads and needed to make choices that I was afraid would be wrong. I went to a quiet place and sat still with one intention: to get clarity. I used surrender in those times of stillness and awaited guidance. Divine wisdom always came soon after in ways I couldn't miss. I became amazed at how wisdom would come in the form of my picking up the right book, seeing the perfect movie, or having the vivid dream needed within a short time. I also used my dreams as a vehicle to attain guidance. Stillness allowed me the room to ask for help and see which tool I should use next.

I still my mouth often in my day, sometimes actually putting my hand over it while in a conversation, so as not to create conflict. As a paid talker, I use words for everything, and it can be obnoxious. Stillness allows others to be right and lets me listen and see them clearly. People are usually asking to be recognized and remembered, so when we acknowledge them by being still and letting them be right or teach us something, they have a chance to shine in our spotlight. My kids have always been insistent on being equals in our relationship, and when they have an answer or skill, I reflect their power in my still presence. I don't remember my dad ever letting me win or be right, and it felt wrong. I can connect to stillness by remembering to plant my feet on the ground and feel my connection to the earth. I can even envision a mountain or a large tree, as I have found that in nature, I can feel safe and at rest. When I practice this tool, I can also receive gifts with head bowed and learn lessons with less resistance. I can meditate to gain stillness or just sit and watch my mind. I have rarely had a still natural mind, but I have enjoyed watching my mind from a still place. There is a sacred, still altar within both true neutrality and all the watcher tools. I feel this still place in the beat of my spiritual heart. The spiritual heart is my oasis from my dualistic human heart, which is alive with love and hate and with separation and connection options. The Self is always at peace, exists in nonduality, and is sustained by the energy of unconditional love. Stillness is one of the bridge tools that connect us to our essence or completeness.

The doing aspect of stillness can help with socially awkward moments when we don't want to appear too helpful or aloof. I just say a simple phrase, such as "How can I be of help?" and remain still, awaiting instructions. Many of us force our help on others and diminish their integrity in doing so. I once used this tool as I was walking to the hospital on a cold morning. I observed a semiparalyzed man getting out of his car to retrieve his wheelchair from the back of his SUV. I stood in his line of sight and became still, as if stating, "I'm here if needed." He went about getting the chair out and fixing his seat. As he was about to leave, he asked me to reach up and close the trunk of his car. Once that was accomplished, he wheeled next to me with a spring of pride in his pace and a kind word on his lips.

Stillness gives us a neutral area to be kind or to use other tools to change a situation or ourselves. This tool is also good for those of us who are better at doing something than just being present. I especially had to learn how to value my still state of being. The tool of stillness gave me a chance to catch my breath and just be.

The quieter you become, the more you can hear.
—Baba Ram Doss

CHAPTER 16
SELF-FILLED SERVICE

What you project or extend is real for you.
—A Course in Miracles

Through the use of spiritual tools, such as humility, honesty, and the forgiveness mind, I began to love myself as a divine project. I noticed how frequently grace touched me, and when I looked back on my life, I saw that I never had been void of love. As my natural mind entertained this foreign concept with more courage and my divine mind became more prevalent, I felt safer and more peaceful. I then began to believe I was a divine being with more certainty, which helped me sustain self-love longer and with more resiliency. I incorporated and used the tools of compassion and unconditional love toward myself to reinforce this concept. This new lens of self-love is now my impetus for service to others.

As the emergence of Self became more powerful, I naturally began teaching myself ways to honor and extend compassion through service to others. I first began service to the suffering with loving gentleness but was still attacking myself for a harm-filled discussion with a motorist or a mean word to a fellow worker, for example. At the time, I didn't realize my wholeness would be the lens by which to see others' needs. I originally gauged my fluctuating self-value by doing good deeds and holding them up against my mistakes. I tallied the score and either rewarded myself with happiness or punished myself with shame and guilt. I was giving service to get good feelings, which I then extended to others. The difficulty was that I still felt fundamentally empty and separated. In retrospect, I realized I was filling a void by doing service. Self-filled service gave me the greatest gift: myself.

With self-filled service, I could see the beauty of love in my essence as it showed through the use of my naturally healing nature in my service to others. I noticed how each action was a glimpse into Self's loving potential. This new vision-correction tool of self-filled service gave me the accurate mirror of the personal self's transformation into higher consciousness that I had been searching for since childhood. I no longer saw myself as needing to earn worthiness and soon became awake to the core of beauty already existing in my loving intention to serve others. I still was discerning as to their behavior and needs but saw all people as one family of evolving souls at different stages of consciousness.

During the first decade of my service to others, I was able to create much love and healing, but I was still void of a consistent peace unless my service was accepted and praised. I became aware of my need to be seen as helpful or effective. When this need wasn't met, I would people-please or retaliate in arrogance and judgment. I needed to be appreciated for my service, and if that did not happen, I felt that separation acutely, and my shame was ignited. It took me years of feeling this shame to realize that the people I helped were not creating my bad feelings by not honoring my service; I was creating the negative feelings. Self-filled service can happen only once we become aware of our intention to use service for selfish means and intend to stop working from the agenda of self-validation. Once I was able to uncover this self-serving style of service, I then could practice new intentions based on my healed perception of personal self. This happened only once I truly saw myself as whole and finally saw love as a constant presence and my life as a work in progress.

This tool of service keeps us learning about how best to love other people by examining what they need, not just fulfilling our needs. Sometimes service takes the form of not helping or just listening. Once I was not invested in the outcome of service, I automatically gave respect to others personal struggles and aspirations. I no longer saw others only as occasions for me to heal; I recognized they were on a sacred pathway for their own awakening. This vision-correction tool unites us and reminds us of the many ways to be in communion with others. The art of listening and humble service are also two great ways to give.

I once was a hospice volunteer while in the military and was assigned to a terminally ill, impoverished twenty-four-year-old man in rural Georgia. On the first visit, I was surprised when he asked me to clean his house, which included a dirty bathroom and kitchen. I was most surprised when he asked me to move his furniture as if he were positioning his bed to face the window with the best view. I kept trying to talk to him about his grief and his faith, but all he did was order me around the house. I actually never got to speak to him deeply about my beliefs, especially my faith in the afterlife, and felt that this client was not a good fit.

I asked the supervisor to take me off the case. Thankfully, she laughed at me, saying, "You'll see. This is a perfect fit for you."

I later realized he had asked me to set up a place for him to die, and my work was a sacred act. I'd carried out my intention to make a difference in his life through my physical labor.

Service can be done through prayer as well. At that time, I viewed prayer as an extension of compassionate love through contemplation or action. I now realize that prayer, as a state of spiritual intention, can take any form. It's not what you do that makes a prayer; it's how and why you do it. My present styles of prayer run the gamut from mundane activities, such as manual labor, to doing sacred rituals as a way to pray for others. Once I became cognizant of the understanding that I was already a whole person, the revelation reminded me that all I needed was already available. That awareness removed an obstacle and revealed the knowledge that service could be a way of loving myself. In loving others, I was actually acting from my loving Self.

I have seen many people give more to others and leave themselves less. Many of these people feel like martyrs or victims eventually and become weary, and they cite these feelings in verbal conflicts to manipulate with guilt. I realized that love extended from Self is increased, never diminished, through service. If we nourish the personal self first, we have more energy to feed others and will then have much better clarity to see appropriate styles of service than if we deprive ourselves. When we are out of balance with service and extend more, we create lack in the personal self. This limiting style often can be fertile ground for physical illness.

This tool is distinctive in the recognition that all people give service creatively in unique styles. When we dare to be new in extending our service to others, we might enjoy the beauty of communion in ways that are an art form. I once released an elderly client from suffering by letting him tell me the same story about his wife for hours, until he broke down in tears and cried, "I'm sorry, my love!" in my arms. I said nothing. It soon became evident to me that in healing others, we heal ourselves.

A teacher once said we should have patience with all things but chiefly have patience with ourselves. I have recently worked hard not to lose courage in considering my own imperfections, and I set about remedying them every day. Because of my previous feelings of lack and an unconscious sense of entitlement, I always lacked patience. I felt like a man without enough air and lived my life awaiting rescue from an outside savior. Practicing patience came in many forms but mostly from observing my own behavior. I soon noticed I spent much of my time protecting and caring for a personal self that constantly felt abandoned and deprived. The vision-correction device of patented patience allows me to stand still enough to see the abundance and loving care around my work. I saw myself as not good enough until I viewed my life through the lens of spiritual vision of Self. The tools of forgiveness and gratitude helped me to correct my insane belief that I had done something bad to deserve to be without love and live in lack in general.

Patented patience is a powerful tool that shows the unfolding of divine intention. The tools of faith and surrender then allow us to wait for what we request until all conditions are ready. My natural mind wanted things on its terms because it believed it was taking care of me without God. My natural belief streams kept reminding me that I had to go out and get everything, not simply ask once and live my life in love and joy. *Patented* means to be secure and to be certain in safety, and *patience* means to allow and be open. I often practice taking a breath and holding it as long as I can to get used to the energy of patience. I have to allow my lungs to absorb and use the ingested air in its time, not mine. I focus on how the body works in digestion and breathing to contemplate patience. I am often at the mercy of its healing timetable, not my life's agenda. In our allowing the body to heal from anything correctly, patience is often tested. I used the words *Just surrender* to allow for patience to be triggered in my mind, emotions, and physical body. I often noticed myself taking short breaths—a symbolic action for the belief that air could run out. I also used to eat quickly, and people commented that I ate as if it were my last meal. I now practice eating slowly, as if there is no hurry or lack of supply.

We should practice patience daily as the world strains to live up to our limited templates of how things should be. Patience allows us to learn from the way life is and doesn't use our energy in manipulating or cutting corners to get what we think we need now. Patented patience is an especially loving vision-correction device in relationships. The more I accepted my own humanness through tolerance and gratitude, the more I could insert simple kindness in relationships. I could then contemplate surrendering my template of how other people had to act. Patience allows events to unfold as gifts. We need to open all gifts if we are to enjoy their benefits. Without patience, we might leave these gifts half opened or discard them. I came to realize eventually as I grew into Self that life is a gift of grace through creation. Even suffering is part of the dualistic plan of contrast learning, as we need suffering to fully know joy on earth. Patience helps us wait through suffering to see the gifts that become more transparent as we heal. I grew much in compassionate intention from my own suffering through the use of patented patience.

There was a time in my career when I was negatively triggered by patients who were extremely dependent. Through supervision and therapy, I came to learn that because I had taken care of myself from an early age, I judged dependency as weakness, which then made being in the presence of severe dependency uncomfortable. To heal from this therapeutic obstacle, I once stayed in therapeutic alliance with a very dependent client, whom I usually would have referred to another professional, for three years. Toward the end of the third year, I healed my own self-judgment and became a better healing force in the client's recovery. It became painfully clear that my negative judgment of my own dependency came from my inner resentment toward my parents for not being safe enough to depend on. My alliance with this brave patient, and his patience with my struggle, became one of the most healing alliances I ever stayed in. I had patience with this client's dependency because of his openness, innocence, and neediness, and I found strength to self-heal because of it. I soon realized that behind what I had judged as apparent neediness was a great soul in need.

We can also practice patented patience during mundane times, such as in traffic, at home, with kids, or at work. All we must do is focus on allowance and stillness as events unfold. Patience also slows down time so as not to create uncomfortable boredom or frustration. Patience is a decision, and once we can incorporate it into our toolbox, we become a beacon of safety for others to heal and feel loved. This tool, like the others, is more powerful when used in tandem with another tool. I used gratitude particularly to increase my patience. I constantly stayed in the moment through being thankful for what was in front of me at the time. This helped keep my natural mind's longing for bigger, better, and quicker at bay until patience was in place. I often use sitting meditation with a focus on serene nature scenes and calm music to help inspire the energy of patience. To better understand the tool of patience, I also contemplate the changing seasons and how long it took to create the universe's natural beauty. I eventually concluded that patience could achieve more than force, and when used in balanced tandem, it mimics all creative endeavor.

The serenity prayer is a spiritual tool in constant use by millions as they attempt to use spiritual technology to negotiate their lives and control the natural mind's penchant for fear, anger, and addiction. Use of this mantra-like prayer strongly utilizes the vision-correction device called discernment. When we are in our perceptual cloudiness, we often cannot see the best choice available at the time and go about creating our lives based on half-truths or past unhealed programming. Discernment comes from the activation of our frontal lobe and our attachment to harmless, compassionate templates of beliefs about us and the world. I recently read a book by Dr. Joe Dispenza called *Breaking the Habit of Being Yourself*, in which he comments that when the frontal lobe is energized, we exhibit our highest, most heightened level of consciousness, our clearest self-awareness and ability to observe reality. This part of our brain is best seen in our ability to discern our world with love and harmlessness.

One Friday after work, I jumped into my Corvette and headed out of the hospital toward the waiting ferry to my vacation island. I got stuck behind an older man in a big sedan who wore dreaded eye-appointment goggles. I would have to follow him for about three miles as we traversed mountain-like single-lane roads on the way to the parkway. My first reaction was anger, which activated my self-centered impatience. My next judgment was that he was an obstacle of injustice. I then wanted to cross the double yellow line and fly by with a surge of big engine power. I then, through grace alone, compassionately thought of him possibly driving fearfully after his procedure. In addition, passing was illegal because of the double yellow line. My next thought was to push him to move from his steady pace of twenty-two miles per hour by tailgating. I realized by his tight grip on the wheel that he was a bit scared and probably struggling to focus, so I backed off. I then thought about backing off more and practicing kindness, but my mind was still agitated, and my emotions screamed that I was the victim of the slow guy. I finally backed off and used mighty discernment to choose the highest thought and subsequent action possible. I chose to back off and hold a loving, protective space through sending him love from a safe distance. I could still be close enough to help but far enough not to put pressure on his anxious adventure. He quickly pulled over onto a safe street and fixed his glasses, and thus, I was on my way to happy hour at the beach. I realized that the four options possible in that situation were only possible through three distinct steps in mighty discernment.

The first step in using this tool is focus. To focus on anything, we must push feelings and self-centered cravings out of the way to look clearly at the situation at hand. To focus means to stay in the present for that instant and look at ramifications and possible outcomes in an instant. This phase changes our attention from the emotions to the intellect in the frontal lobe. I call it "*I* over *E*," as opposed to the normal "*E* over *I*" formula the natural mind uses to manipulate the environment for pleasure. I often call in the mighty tool of discernment by saying out loud, "*I* over *E*."

The next phase is discernment proper. In this step, we entertain the whole situation and then play the tape through in our head. For example, when I wanted to pass the old gentleman at first, I envisioned a police officer in my head, and then I saw him giving a ticket. Through compassion, I also considered what the man might feel when scared by the roar of an unexpected engine burst when I passed him. These divine-minded thoughts were not driven by the unchecked self-centered emotions that most likely would have made a hasty choice.

The third part of the tool is choice. I made a choice for the harmless good and was quickly rewarded by the man's turning off the road. Mighty discernment is a vision-clarity device that allows us to choose the higher thought and its subsequent words and actions. This tool minimizes shame and guilt, because the choice includes others in mind and allows us to stay compassionate.

I originally began to teach these three steps—focus, discernment, and choice—knowingly but eventually was able to incorporate them into my interactions with others. The other powerful part of using this device is the impact it has on the law of cause and effect in our lives. I am becoming more aware of this perfect teacher in my life, much as an analogy of my golf game illustrates. If I make a hasty shot and the ball ends up in the woods, the next shot is harder. If I prepare and use discernment skills to hit the ball safely, the subsequent shots are usually easier, and thus, my mission is accomplished with minimal effort.

The practical ability to use this device begins and ends with practice. I had to consciously interject these three steps into all endeavors of my life for a while, even when I felt as though it took away spontaneity. For me, this was good because when I acted impulsively apart from my loving template of compassion, I primarily acted out of a fear-filled, self-serving place. I also used existing positive models to implement the new template into daily practice. I used the self-talk phrase "What would Jesus, Buddha, Muhammad, Krishna, or Baal Shem do?" to determine how I believed a higher-conscious being would act, and I followed suit. These examples of ascended masters are unique to me, and whom I chose had only to do with what I was reading or learning at the time. Mighty discernment activates my creative mind as it brings blood flow to the frontal lobe and stimulates my imagination. I am then left in awe and gratitude for choices I made that were loving and compassionate. These choices, when held against the emotionally impulsive history of past choices that resulted in meanness or hurtfulness through ignorance, felt like a new power source and resource of Self inspiration. The result of using mighty discernment is always more peace and joy. This mighty tool gave me social fearlessness and more compassionate service while diminishing my guilt and shame.

It is interesting to observe how a character defect can become a strength once we become aware of it. I often have the need to obsess over a problem until it is resolved. Over the years, I transformed this once neurotic tendency into thought streams that were analytical and revelatory. I was able to progress to a more present state of peace and contentment by taking inventory regularly. When my emotions were showing me I was out of alignment with Self and I felt disunity, I would use single-minded devotion to search out why. Through years of self-study and formal psychotherapeutic training, I concluded that I had four distinct bodies that needed attention.

I was always taught to take care of my physical body, and as a collegiate athlete, I brought my training to levels that gave me much success. The physical body I learned to care for had its bumps and lumps but was a faithful traveler and communicator.

I also became aware from my childhood pain that my emotional body was truly a force to reckon with. The majority of my pain from childhood came from my parents' toxic relationship, and I carried their shame and my fears in this emotional body.

The next body to come into play was my mental body, with all its fear-filled beliefs and insecurities about my future. I seemed to be able to control this body least in my teens, as

I lived impulsively through the emotional body and did little introspection.

Growing up religious, I always had a relationship with the God of my religion. I had a picture on my wall and rituals that reminded me of divine love. This was the foundation for my spiritual body.

Becoming aware of these important life players eventually led me to develop a state of balance to have harmony. The escort tool called ballistic balance is the distribution of love, attention, and wellness to all four bodies daily. I used this tool as I paid specific attention to each body's needs and attended to the balancing of the whole being through loving attention.

I always exercised and practiced good hygiene as a kid and a teen, but college saw my physical body abused a bit through experimentation and a lack of attention to minor pains and illness. During college, there was no supervision, and my body suffered along with me as I found my limitations and boundaries through pain and illness. The following suggestions are best practices I use to stay in balance for each of the four bodies.

A. Physical

1. Exercise three to five times weekly.
2. Practice daily hygiene.
3. Maintain physical contact with others through intimacy, play, and therapeutic massage.
4. Maintain contact with nature.
5. Keep up with medical commitments, such as check-ups, medications, and dental work.
6. Be mindful of dietary adjustments and healthy eating.

The emotional body craves attention constantly through sundry feelings and vibrations. This body is often the most neglected because of our ignorance about emotional states and what they communicate to the other bodies. For example, I came to see that my father's low emotional IQ left him with two feelings: anger and happiness. He was ignorant of how his body worked and, subsequently, couldn't teach me the language of feelings, which left me unequipped to negotiate life without a lot of mistakes and pain. The emotional body is also a great asset in realizing whether we are aligned with Self or not. When we are suffering emotionally, it's as if we are being called to heal and move through our tools into centeredness.

B. Emotional

1. Know about feelings. Learn what they are and what they communicate about who we are and what we believe.
2. Keep a journal to externalize the feelings of the day in an attempt to relieve their pressure and learn what they are teaching.
3. Frequently share feelings with someone you trust, whether in written letters, verbal words, art, or poetry. This can be done in prayer on a constant basis.
4. Allow all feelings to surface safely through awareness before repressing them or acting on them.
5. Use several of the tools to get your delay mechanism in place and working.
6. Exercise. This can relieve stress once the emotion is recognized. Do not exercise without introspection and analysis, though, or you run the risk of repressing the emotional messenger.

The next body is a favorite of many who like figuring things out through thoughts and bypassing emotions. The mental body, which includes the natural and divine minds, is our helpful guardian, as it makes logic and wisdom the redeemer of ignorance and expresses lessons in manageable language to be learned and taught. The mental body is especially powerful as we negotiate our world of needs, drives, and pleasures. The following endeavors are designed to utilize the full potential of our mental capacity and stimulate positive neural network pathways in our brains.

C. Mental

1. Use the techniques of mental rehearsal, attention, and ritual. We create new neural networks in new patterns and thus create communities of neurons to wire together in new combinations, creating a new level of mind. I call these vision-correction tools.
2. Learn more about how to better focus your thoughts through meditation or thought-training techniques, including guided imagery.
3. Implement positive thoughts of a loving, nonjudgmental nature into your daily cognitive script.
4. Replace outdated negative belief systems and slogans by observing them on your mind screen and saying, for example, "Cancel!" or "That's not me!" Write them in your journal to achieve clarity and distance in order to change their energy.
5. Realize that each thought affects your body one one-hundredth of a second before it becomes conscious. Patterns of negative thoughts affect our physical bodies over time.

The next body is one that most people don't delineate as a specific body, but most alternative healing literature refers to it as an alternative group of thoughts and practices for wellness.

It became evident to me over time that the spiritual body not only created my state of peace but also was the catalyst for a deeper desire to evolve into a more compassionate person. In my experience, my spiritual body is a system of healing energy that affects all other bodies directly. I have found that by doing specific spiritual practices, I bring about major positive effects on the other three bodies. I have also found that by negating this body, people have become spiritually bankrupt, and this has had a profound negative impact on the other three bodies.

D. Spiritual

1. Meditate with the spiritual intention to be in communion with the higher power or to just be still.
2. Carry out prayer, ritual, or sacred practice with the intention to be in communion with a loving, forgiving energy.
3. Do activities that involve service to nature or others with the intention to love.
4. Contemplate spiritual concepts, truths, or occasions to gain revelation and peace through focus.
5. Use dietary habits designed to honor a higher purpose or intention.
6. Be a member of a spiritual community.

By doing these things daily and creating balance, we bring out the innate peace, joy, and wellness that are our right as loving people. Balance in all bodies brings peace, and peace is the gateway to bliss.

CHAPTER 17
ABUNDANT GENEROSITY

*We were right we were giving. That's how
we kept what we gave away.*
—**Neil Young, "Comes a Time"**

I grew up in a family who felt the constant fear of lack. From an early age, I was taught that we lacked money, and that manifested in fights between my parents. I also felt my father was withholding money and material things. He didn't do this to hurt me, but he lived in fear of not having enough. He would withhold the use of his car or say he didn't have enough time to play with me. My mom always felt my father withheld love and attention, and thus, they lived in a relationship that was cold and angry. I needed the tool of abundant generosity desperately as I grew older, due to my resultant fear of not having enough love, money, time to myself, and, especially, peace of mind. The dark teacher of lack affected my social style and eventually created a persona I didn't like. As I grew older, I became generous as I started to have more faith in the law of abundance.

The vision-correction tool called abundant generosity takes faith to a new level. To give first without expectation of return on our terms is the first principle. I had to learn to give first and release fully or await return in God's time, not mine. I practiced this tool for several years, and I continue to consciously return to it as a refresher. I began by looking into the laws of attraction and reading books directly related to faith and manifestation practices. I then began to dismantle my old beliefs from childhood that kept me shackled to lack and unworthiness. Because of this fruitful learning, I started to believe that all I needed had already been granted, and it was the law.

I knew that my responsibility was to stay in the vortex of Self as much as I could at all times. I wrote out a wish list of desires and put it in the form of an invocation. Many mystics and spiritual beings manifest their needs through this type of prayer. I wrote things like the following: "I have material abundance," "I am a powerful healer and speaker," and "I am a patient, loving dad and husband." I wrote these templates in the present, as if they were already true. I then added constant use of the tool of gratitude as I recognized all the things I had already. Finally, I used surrender as a way to allow the spirit to do its work.

I recently began to look for occasions to be generous in all ways. I give money to the needy, compliments to people who are used to being ignored, and love through attention to my four bodies and to others in my life. I do this without focusing on my action's return in the form of unidirectional extension. As stated earlier, this style of extension means that my only concern is to give; I do not concern myself with receipt. I also came to realize that the universe circulates abundance throughout the earth, and when I give anything of value in life, it only multiplies.

This allowed my vision of the world and God to change once I practiced this tool. I no longer saw the world or God as doling out money, relationships, or success; rather, I believed I could manifest all I needed through action and faith. I also used this tool to practice letting go of attachment to material things.

Recently, I bought a new car and went through painstaking ways to keep it safe from dings and dents. At the two-month mark, my eight-year-old son opened the family truck door and put a major ding in my new car. I initially got angry and pouted about the car, until he piped up and said, "I thought people were more important than things." He reminded me to let go and get over it.

I have reverence for all things, but material attachment brings only pain and revenge. I stand now with hands open and in the flow of universal grace called abundance. I don't hold on too tightly with fear but allow all things to pass to people downstream through generous acts and donations. This book is an act of generosity to others and to myself, and as I give away my life lessons as a way for others to achieve new vision and see life in peace and love, I am becoming more conscious of my own Self.

As I learn in the newness of clarity because of these steps, there are times that seem dark and sad on the spiritual path. I am writing this book in the midst of a pandemic. As a healer, during these lonely and dangerous times, I am always acutely aware of the need for hope. I saved this tool for last because it is my constant companion. As a child, I often felt hopeless, especially in my ability to change my parents' relationship and their suffering. I kept trying to move them to love each other, behaving in ways to make them happy and learning new words to give them inspiration to continue our family. I first realized I had hope when I began to make lists of possible things to say to get them to forgive each other. I wrote these inspirational thoughts down as if to make them real, and the lists became a hope-filled template to continue the tough mission of keeping my family together.

I began to teach about hope when I first worked with teenage drug addicts at an outreach center. I quickly saw that my one constant topic was maintaining hope and realized how setting out a grid to secure hope could ignite its loving touch. As my career took shape and paralleled my personal healing from shame, I began to use the tool of hope in all areas of my life. I saw it as a beacon of light in what seemed like a long tunnel of suffering. I first envisioned hope as a grid after a session with my teacher, who discussed hope's grid-like strength in our lives. I pictured the wire support structure that is put down to support concrete when it is being poured into preformed grids. I then started to see that hope is a structure but not the strengthening agent behind completion. This is where action comes in.

I kept remembering what a professor had told me about Sigmund Freud's work being summed up in two human needs: love and work. I started to write down behavioral, cognitive, and intentional changes in a grid structure drawn on paper. This grid represented the love part of hope as I acted out my resolution and self-affirming intention to move forward. The power to work for change is found in resolve and intention. The structure is strong and allows for many options. Once this grid is in place, I use my mental body and spiritual body to fill in the tools needed to accomplish the work part. The tools can be a place to aspire to, a quality of behavior, or a dream put into word form. My dream of becoming a social worker drove me daily in school and the military and kept me focused. The grid could include any mental, physical, emotional, and spiritual thoughts or activities I believed would help complete love's hope-filled vision of my becoming a professional social worker. The emotional body brought up the strength found in courage and desire. I then began by placing realistic thoughts and activities that could bring me out of hopelessness and into success or revelation.

The following is the grid I used to become a social worker after I had been turned down from my only graduate school application.

My Hope Grid

A. Army basic training as a medic and further counseling training in behavioral science training schools in San Antonio, Texas, and Fort Sam, Houston
B. Army education scholarship to pay for graduate school
C. Professional reading
D. Volunteer work as hospice worker
E. New professional friends
F. Hard study
G. Spiritual ritual daily
H. Training and work as crisis counselor
I. Volunteer work at orphanage
J. Master's degree in social work
K. Love of myself in all bodies to keep balance
Be a powerful healer.

As you can see, I outlined specific ways to form a path to my goal, which was always written at the bottom of the page. I did all these things and kept this written grid in my head as I went through my day. This hope-filled toolbox was the template for all my actions on personal, spiritual, and professional levels.

With this concrete tool, we can negotiate and conquer the pain-filled areas of apathy and despair. These nonproductive residual feelings were powerful teachers, as they prompted me to movement and awakening. This grid was a rope thrown out as a lifeline in a dark future based on childhood beliefs in lack and projected failure. I could constantly update and adjust the activities on the grid to reflect my present financial status and living arrangement. I was always able to go back to the grid to reinforce belief in my success. The grid kept my intention to be a loving person and healer in focus for me in times when my emotional body and mental state were mired in darkness. This vision-correction device helped me to change numerous blockages and painful lessons into awakenings and material to help others. I am still always inspired by the practice and tool of hope.

In conclusion, I have come to realize that my experiences were ultimately powerful occasions to uncover the many essential qualities that lie dormant in Self. I use these tools over and over again as I teach them to countless others. I now believe the greatest way to help others is to show them my life working well. These tools were the change agents that facilitated my spiritual character and professional success. I am a living example that the use of these divine character-building tools will have life-changing positive effects on everything in your life. I see a new earth emerging, and by using these both new and ancient tools, we can expedite the birth of the Self asleep in us all.

The natural mind, with its personal shell of self, will eventually not need vision correction, because we will see only through what we have become. From the clarity of neutral witness to the use of surrender and humility, one can walk the spiritual path with more faith in its destination. Through the immutable laws of duality and cause and effect, we can see the direction in which we are heading, and as we learn the skills of balance and discernment, we can create a life beyond one previously hoped for. When we look out through the eyes of forgiveness, our thinking can see the Self in contrast to our personal limitations, and in the beauty of the earth school, we can listen to our lives with the ears of unconditionality and inhale a breath of joy. Please understand that the use of any tool or escort device will have positive effects on your life. We must only stay the course on our own sacred journey to transform into a living presence of Self. As we lay aside the garment of the personal self as master and the natural mind as keeper, our lives can truly become gifts for the greater good.

∞

No longer do I live, but it is Christ who lives in me.
—Saint Paul

QUESTIONS AND ANSWERS

I realized the following section was necessary after years of entertaining questions on the topic of spiritual technology and the path to the Self. Please look through the questions to see if they pique your interest or can serve to further clarify concepts that seemed either interesting or vague. Be aware that this section will go over previously mentioned tools and concepts as it reiterates the importance of repetition in this type of learning.

Q: How do these tools work?

A: These tools come from existing potentials in our lives. For example, kindness comes from an existing energy called pleasantness in the world. Each tool has a core of power already existing in it. Practicing a tool is like taking a vitamin for the body; once we make the choice to take it, it does the work out of its existing and predetermined capacity. Our job in using these healing energies is to set the intention to incorporate their energy into ourselves and then work to embody their ingredients in our minds, beliefs, feelings, and bodies with repetition and creativity. Each tool works to the level of our capacity to learn and practice its formula. The tool will eventually move from knowledge to belief and then from voluntary to involuntary use. This happened to me with attitudinal gratitude. I started out by forcing myself to be thankful until I developed a habit of saying thank-you for all things received. It only takes the practice of one tool to change your life. The use of even one tool over time will lessen the control of the programming of the natural mind, just as pulling one strand from a rug will unravel it completely in time. This lessening of the past unveils the higher states of consciousness already existing in our divine potentialities. My personal path showed me that in the beginning, while practicing the tools, I was more willing to put effort into using a tool when I was in pain. I found that my mistakes or stuck points were open doors for new technology. I found I would put more time into practice and contemplation because it would keep me from feeling hopeless and negative. The tools will help with suffering or enhance existing states of joy. They are productive in all light or dark situations.

Q: What other hints would you give to help spiritual seekers better utilize the tools?

A: I found that meditation for ten to twenty minutes in the morning helped me to focus the tool in my conscious mind for the day. I practiced a form of meditation called contemplation, which consisted of using a specific tool as a creative thought endeavor. In a quiet place, I would imagine myself using the tool and being the tool and would think of positive outcomes brought about by its incorporation into my life. These outcomes usually took the form of abundance of money, positive relationship experiences, or a creative healing force during my work with others.

Q: When should I use the tools?

A: You are probably already using these tools in one form or another but without focus or appreciation. I found that by naming them specifically and seeing them as technology, I could automatically look to the toolbox for help in crisis situations. For example, I use total tolerance constantly to deal with crisis situations in my home. My children constantly kick up my feelings from childhood as they make loud noises and create chaos. I automatically react to these situations with fear and anger. I use total tolerance to breathe through my extreme feelings and fill my mind with thoughts of allowance and safety. This helps me be a better parent. I also use radical humility as a daily practice to evolve as a therapist and teacher. I use certain tools socially and others privately. There is a tool for the amelioration of every situation. By using these tools consciously with the intention to be the best person possible, you will have many occasions to practice their power in your life. I attempt to be the best I am in all I do.

Q: A popular saying is "Be careful what you ask for." Will the use of these tools bring forth problems in my life that weren't there before?

A: I don't have more problems now that I am half awake, but I consciously take responsibility for them. They don't get denied or become a crisis as often. I recontextualized my view of my life from the victim role to the creator role. As the victim, I was blocking punches and moving quickly out of pain only to have the pain pop up again and again. As a creator, I am challenged to use my skills and spiritual, emotional, and mental strengths to be creative in all endeavors. I have new glasses on, and they maintain my hope. I did encounter relationship changes as I became more awake, due to the need to be around like-minded people. I also found that I didn't have to gather suffering people around me to try to fix them in order to feel good. I just stopped enabling them, and they faded. I did find that I had to adjust my social chatter to each person's ability to hear spiritual-based words and receive love through deeper discussions. I had to relearn how to talk in mundane ways and practice total tolerance often while I went through an arrogant, egoistic spiritualized stage. I realized I felt somehow better than because I was spiritually astute. Through radical humility and discernment, I am becoming flexible in all social occasions.

Q: Are there any side effects from using these tools?

A: In the beginning, I experienced periods of impatience and disappointment because I was looking for immediate changes. My natural mind was mimicking being spiritual as it constantly saw fit to judge my progress. It actually was trying to dictate my changes and wanted peace, joy, and abundance too soon. I also had to see the blockages to my progress as resistances from my preexisting belief system. I had to go back into my dark beliefs about myself and others as well as my outdated relationship with God. All these inadequate and pain-reinforcing beliefs had to be updated. For example, my belief in lack was a block I had to face and overcome by using abundant generosity. I had to reprogram my worthiness belief and update it to say to myself, "I am worthy of all things because of my innate goodness." You must be brave as you look at your beliefs that limit and create destruction. This can be seen as painful, but it is all a matter of your willingness to do so. My purpose was to get out of the existing hell I was in, so I was willing to experience it again with all the help available in my tools and the love around me. Pain shared is pain lessened.

Q: Are relationships going to change once I utilize these tools?

A: Relationships are always my mirrors and teachers. I find they reflect changes in relationships or needed changes in myself. I had to let go of certain negative relationship patterns, such as people-pleasing and neediness, and the people who needed me in those roles were upset and uncomfortable. I had to have total tolerance for my changes and for others' right to end relationships when they were uncomfortable. I also began to see relationships as either dark teachers or light teachers. Dark teachers were in my life so I could look into aspects of myself that were painful. Dark teachers came from relationships in which people judged and rejected me and I compromised myself, not staying truthful to myself or them. A lot of my tools were used in this lesson. I constantly felt judged and rejected. I perfected a lot of tools during dark relationships at work and with my family. Light relationships are people who are models of a tool or are loving, supportive, safe people in our lives. I actually learned much more about unconditional love from pets and nature than from people. These wonderful mirrors were great light teachers in my life. People can play either dark or light teachers, depending on what happens. My kids and wife especially depend on the work I do to evolve from the mirrors shown to me daily. All relationships are perfect for our evolution, no matter what they bring. I learned to let go of people from the past whom I didn't seem to resonate with. I loved them all in my heart but didn't need the lessons they taught any longer. There is no reason to linger in relationships unless they continue to teach you or serve to help you evolve in love. It is also arrogant to think that other people can't help someone as well as we do. I eventually realized the beliefs that people need us and that we should socially compromise our joy by staying in abusive relationships to help others were natural-mind tricks to get false value. We can always just send prayer and move to a more self-honoring place either physically or mentally to get enough distance to get clarity.

Q: Is there a specific daily formula by which to incorporate the tools into my routine?

A: I begin with meditation, which is a ten-minute period to quiet my loud ego mind. My natural mind tells me in the morning, "Something's wrong," "You did something bad," "You don't have enough," or "It's going to be a tough day." I sit in stillness and cleanse my thoughts through deep breathing until I get my watcher in charge. My watcher is always more powerful and more loving than my mind. I then choose a tool I was working on or a new tool and intend to use it. I say out loud or write in my journal, "I am total tolerance," or some other tool. I say it as if it is already completely in my energy. I then contemplate what the tool means in terms of energy, meaning, and behavior. I look for occasions to practice it in my thoughts and actions throughout the day. At times, I put it into my journal if the lesson is particularly tough or if the tool is foreign to my existing behavior and belief system. Then I surrender it to the divine to set up my day perfectly for the practice of all my tools.

Q: How do I keep motivated to use my toolbox?

A: I found that being aware of the little victories won during the struggle of the day helps. I allow myself to keep going, no matter how I feel. I don't judge the progress I am making but only evaluate the effort I put in and the speed with which I identify the tool I need to use. I saw over the years that even though I still felt bad, others saw me changing. My natural mind is good at hiding the good stuff I do from my watcher. I also allow love to be shown back to me from all sources. My own vision of my effort, love from others, success in work, and especially the recognition of joy and peace as a state of being kept me striving for more solid states of happiness not contingent on outside stimuli. I also have an imperative to keep my promises to myself. When I take on a new tool, it is as if I've hired a trainer and promised him my effort and commitment. When I don't follow through, I feel guilt and shame appropriately, so I get back to work. I used to give up under the weight of shame and guilt, but as I have integrated them into my life as helpers, not punishers, I feel lighter and learn lessons more quickly.

Q: When should I teach my tools to people I think can benefit from them?

A: I am a teacher by profession and attempt daily to use my life experiences with the tools to help others. I've also found that by teaching them to people who are interested, I learn them better. I give it away to keep it. I have also found that people are sensitive to being taught anything. It kicks up their shame, so I only teach them from the perspective of my own struggle. I am sensitive not to say, "You should try this," or "Try this." I am a searcher, as they are, and I constantly try to use radical humility as a reminder to let people be where they are. The greatest way to pass on love is to model it working well in our lives. Spirituality is best served by attraction, not preaching.

Q: How many tools can I use at once?

A: I take on one tool at a time formally but am awake to daily opportunities to use the other tools. I use a tool a week formally and switch tools constantly as the need arises. Also, it is important to use tools that seem to fit easily rather than those that seem like too much effort. You have a choice to force a tool into your life, but in doing so, you could become discouraged and give up the whole endeavor. For example, I tried to use automatic forgiveness with a colleague at work but found I had to switch to total tolerance quickly. I was simply not willing to surrender my resentments at that level yet. I did eventually forgive after I did more self-forgiveness work. I often thought I got a tool down, until an old situation came back and I found I wasn't able to use the tool automatically. I would then go back to that tool for more work. I always felt I learned better after a mistake or a crisis. I would then have faith that I had done my best and would move on. I also had periods when I consciously did not take on new tools, because I wanted to practice existing tools in new areas. I also have certain tools on board constantly, such as abundant generosity and radical humility. I also use rigorous honesty as a constant companion. These are my imperatives. They make up the triangle of my integrity.

Q: Can I use the tools in my own time and in my own way if I feel I can't follow your formula?

A: These tools are universal energies and gifts from divine love and our best humanity. They are ours to practice creatively. Remember, just the intention to change begins the process. Your journey is unique and perfect for your evolution. I do suggest you learn single-minded devotion as quickly as possible because of the natural mind's tendency to give up on life-changing endeavors.

GLOSSARY OF TERMS

abundance: The energy in the universe that creates the potential of plenty. One could have an abundance of talent, material goods, love, or opportunities.

acrimonious: Mean or acting out of contempt.

agenda: A preplanned intention that gets carried out in real time. A blueprint for the creation of outcome through directed action or unconscious default. One could have a sexual agenda in a relationship.

attraction: An energy in the universe that creates through magnetic resonance. It is stimulated by thoughts and agenda on conscious and unconscious levels. Like attracts like.

awakening: An event or revelation that brings clarity and energy in the form of an epiphany or lessons learned. My heart surgery was an awakening to the preciousness of life.

big dreams: Dreams that have specific messages for revelation. They occur usually between midnight and four o'clock in the morning. These are dreams in which one can see discarnate souls, spiritual teachers, and guides.

character: The way one behaves in the world as an external expression of beliefs, karmic tendencies, and intentions.

communion: The feeling, act, or occasion of spiritual love between two separate entities. I was in communion with the sea on vacation.

contemplation: In-depth investigation through meditation or ritual exercise to further the intimate relationship between a preexisting knowledge base and intuition. The integration of a concept or experience into personal transformation.

clarity: The gift of clear understanding or external vision.

conduit: An open portal for the distribution of energy in various forms. I became a conduit of loving energy in my workplace.

dark teacher: A person, place, or experience that teaches through consequential process. These teachers help us to learn through suffering and hidden lessons.

delay system: A mental concept or physical ritual that allows for better choices by staving off impulsive thoughts or behavior. When I got mad at the kids, I clapped three times to remind myself to be patient.

divine mind: The aspect of Self that is in direct communion with the divine wisdom of the universe or of our personal God. This is the creator of our best thoughts and most loving art and wisdom.

dualism: The predominant learning impetus on earth. One cannot truly know anything without knowing its opposite as well. I couldn't know love without knowing hate. I can't know the Self without living in the contrast of personal self.

essence: The core of the best qualities in each person's character. The divinity within as it is expressed in practical qualities. I have compassion as an essential quality.

externalization: The act of expressing feelings or thoughts that hold repressed power. Talking, writing, singing, or praying in an attempt to either relieve suffering or objectify the internal process. This allows for better inventory and scrutiny of both functional and dysfunctional patterns.

grace: The divine influx of energy from spirit to enhance our lives. This quality of consciousness is omnipresent and ever attending.

guilt: The belief in and subsequent feeling of self-attack on a behavior, thought, or physical attribute ("I hate myself for …"). Healthy guilt is a productive awakening system used by the ego to keep us in good moral direction.

hidden teaching: The lessons found in difficult dualistic struggles. They can be earned from any occasion or person. They can include dark or light teachers. Even physical pain or illness can teach us how to allow love into our lives.

inevitability: The dualistic belief in cause and effect. Spiritually, all things unfold as a result of choices and karmic potential.

internal interaction: The interchange of intellect and watcher. The ability to take and the act of taking personal inventory.

intention: The focus of thought energy and will in a particular direction.

intuition: Instinctive knowing (without the use of rational processes).

karma: The effects of a person's actions that determine his or her destiny. The spiritual law holds to the premise "For every action, there is a reaction." I liken it to the use of a cosmic credit card. If I make a choice that hurts others, self, or nature, I will experience an equally painful lesson in either time or eternity to gain opportunities to progress in consciousness.

light teacher: A person, place, or experience that teaches through love and information.

manipulative device: A natural-mind activity stimulated by dishonesty and craving to obtain a human need. I used people-pleasing to stave off attack.

miracle: Any amazing, wonderful occurrence or revelatory change in thought that has a powerful changing effect on one's life.

natural mind: The dualistic psychic energy system assigned to protect the body by meeting its need for pleasure and security. The programming is based on a paranoid concept of fear and punishment through attack or abandonment. Its only reference to life is through the past and templates of conscious and unconscious thoughts that can create a pseudoimagination. The natural mind believes it is in charge of your life and the origin of your life force. In contrast, spiritual concepts are anathema to its nature.

personal path: Specific ways that life lessons unfold for each unique individual.

potential: The inherent capacity in the universe for coming into being in our lives.

personal self: The self run by the natural mind. It consists of both fixed and flexible character styles and traits. It is the social extension of our humanness, as it carries out primal and social mandates and suggestions. This layer of our life acts like a mediator between our inner world and our outer existence. It is better known as our personality. It is the henchman of the natural mind in that it is our facade as we go about seeking pleasure and minimizing psychic pain in any way the natural mind demands.

recontextualize: To view something in a better way. I use humor to recontextualize people's mistakes.

resentments: Lingering grudges and anger toward people, places, or events.

resonance: Vibratory relationship of mutual understanding or trust and agreement between people. The ability to influence others through our own being.

self-love: The active caring of all aspects of the self (the four self bodies: physical, emotional, mental, and spiritual). This can be a state of being, an activity, or an intention. It can even be sourced from the natural mind's understanding of the value inherent in our own personality.

shame: A painful emotion or state of being resulting from an awareness of inadequacy or guilt.

spiritual technology: Past or present wisdom used in a practical way to make the quality of one's life better. These technologies come from all cultures and paths to spiritual attainment.

surrender: The act of letting go of thoughts, past events, or outcomes.

template: A model or standard for making comparisons.

tool: The means used to accomplish a certain goal or growth-filled task.

toolbox: A cluster of existing tools at one's disposal for immediate or long-term use.

unconscious terms: Expressions we are not aware of stored in the unconscious that can actively affect our thinking. The aspect of our natural mind in which we repress unwanted, traumatic thoughts and events.

vision changers: Insights and revelations that change the concept of self, which then changes the perception of the outside world.

CPSIA information can be obtained
at www.ICGtesting.com
Printed in the USA
BVHW050157090822
644134BV00003B/58